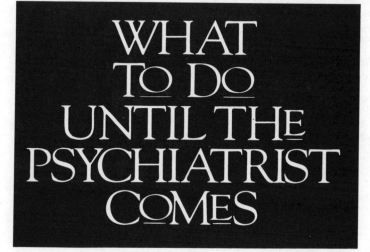

WHAT TO DO UNTIL THE PSYCHIATRIST COMES

BOB PHILLIPS

HARVEST HOUSE PUBLISHERS
Eugene, Oregon 97402

WHAT TO DO UNTIL THE PSYCHIATRIST COMES

Copyright © 1995 by Harvest House Publishers
Eugene, Oregon 97402

Library of Congress Cataloging-in-Publication Data

Phillips, Bob, 1940–
    What to do until the psychiatrist comes / Bob Phillips.
      p. cm.
    Includes bibliographical references and index.
    ISBN 1-56507-231-6
    1. Bible—Psychology—Miscellanea.   2. Psychology and religion—Miscellanea.
    3. Christian life.   4. Spiritual healing—Miscellanea.   I. Title.

BS645.P54 1995
248.8'6—dc20
                                 95-9663
                                 CIP

Printed in the United States of America.

96 97 98 99 00 01 — 10 9 8 7 6 5 4 3 2

To Dr. Henry Brandt and Dr. Jay Adams.
These two men have held high the
importance of the Bible in counseling.
They have coupled sound wisdom with
a sincere desire to help people.
They have personally encouraged and
helped me to think and grow.

Contents

—— *A Word from the Author* ——

*Keep your face to the sunshine
and you cannot see the shadow.*
—Helen Keller*

What a wild time to be alive. It is a time of crisis. Our families and our nation stand at a crossroad of change. The very fabric of our society is under attack. The traditional values that our country was founded upon have been eroded by decades of social change.

The breakdown of the family has increased by dramatic proportions. Crime and drug usage are issues faced even by small-town America. Problems such as AIDS and abortion are dividing communities.

It is difficult, if not impossible, to read newspapers and magazines that do not regale us with murder, betrayal, and disaster. Television is filled with soap operas and talk shows that deal with every possible form of wickedness and sexual deviation.

Not only have the national and international problems increased, but individual difficulties are also on the rise. Billions of dollars are spent annually in dealing with mental health. Tons of barbiturates are consumed daily by people trying to cope with life. Mental hospitals and psychiatric clinics are crowded with hurting people. Suicide is still one of the major causes of death. Nervous breakdowns, stress disorders, and emotional exhaustion are common in many families.

In the Chinese language, there is a symbol for the word *crisis*. It is formed by combining two characters.

One character stands for the concept of danger and the other represents opportunity.

To each is given a bag of tools,
A shapeless mass, and a book of rules,
And each must make, ere life is flown,
A stumbling block, or a stepping-stone.

There is no question that we all face problems and difficulties. Everyone has pressure and pain. But this is part of being included in the human race. How we face our difficulties is what makes or breaks us.

Charles H. Spurgeon said, "Many men owe the grandeur of their lives to their tremendous difficulties." Our attitude toward the stress of life is the key. A. W. Tozer addressed this when he said, "Things are for us only what we hold them to be. Which is to say that our attitude toward things is more likely, in the long run, to be more important than the things themselves."

This book has been born out of the desire to help people change their outlook toward their pressures and difficulties.

Like many young people entering college, I was not sure what profession I would pursue. I enrolled as a Christian Education and Bible major and minored in Psychology. Upon graduation, I joined the staff of an interdenominational Christian ministry, and later I went on to become a licensed minister. I then went back to school and earned an M.A. in Counseling, became a Licensed Marriage, Family, and Child Counselor, and eventually went on for a Ph.D. in Counseling.

After 30 years of ministry and over 12,000 hours of individual counseling with people, I am convinced there are some positive answers for people facing personal and emotional difficulties.

I believe the answers for life's problems are found in the pages of a rule book: the Bible. I make no apologies for this bias. I have personally experienced and witnessed these answers transforming people time and time again. The concepts within the Bible will help you to come to terms with and resolve hurt and pain. They will help you understand your fears, angers, and frustrations. The Bible helps us to deal with guilt, make restitution, and forgive other people. The Bible instructs us how to face death. It teaches us how to find happiness, peace, and joy even in the midst of trouble.

As a counselor, I know that many people do not seek any form of professional advice for their difficulties. They either talk to their friends or try to work out the problems themselves. Often individuals cannot afford the high cost of counseling . . . not to mention the amount of time it requires. For some, they would go for counseling help, but they do not know where to go. They do not know whom they can trust. And counselors may simply not be available.

This book is a modest effort to try and bridge the gap between the high cost of counseling and the unavailability of counselors. It is by no means exhaustive in its scope, nor could any book be. This book is an attempt to touch on the more common problems encountered in counseling and give direction.

Although the book was primarily written for the individual to become his or her own counselor (with God's help), it may be used in other ways. Those leading small group discussions or home studies may want to use it as a guide. Adult Bible classes or laymen who desire to assist in counseling may find it helpful. Ministers or professional counselors may use it as a homework assignment for the individuals they are counseling.

It is my prayer that the reader will be helped, challenged, or confronted by the concepts presented. This book is not written just to assist people in coping with or getting relief from symptoms. It is designed to change readers' perceptions of their problems and start them in a brand-new direction in life.

—Bob Phillips
Fresno, CA

CHAPTER ONE

Am I Crazy?

One out of four people in this country is mentally imbalanced. Think of your three closest friends. If they seem okay, then you're the one.

—Ann Landers

"I feel like I am losing my mind," said Donna as she slumped down in a chair in my office. She began to tell me how she and her husband, Ralph, were having difficulties.

"On Tuesday night after dinner, I noticed that Ralph was very quiet. I asked him what was wrong. He said that nothing was wrong. He then began yelling at the kids for no big reason. I again asked him what was wrong. He said that everything was all right. At bedtime I tried to get him to open up. He said that he was okay and then rolled over and went to sleep. I know something is wrong, but he says there is nothing wrong. He has been acting this way for more than a month. I think I'm going crazy."

Robert also thought that he was going crazy. He shared with me how he lacked self-confidence. He didn't seem to be going anywhere at work and was very unassertive with people. He began to withdraw from social relationships. He avoided large crowds and found that anytime he had to speak, his heart began to pound and his mouth became dry. He thought that he was very abnormal.

Marcy had been feeling depressed for weeks. She had lost her enthusiasm for life. She had the "blahs." She had no energy and felt empty and alone. She found herself withdrawing from family, friends, and life in general. She just didn't feel good. She had even entertained thoughts of ending all the pain by taking her own life. As she broke down and cried she said, "I am a real mental case."

Marcy had recently completed her divorce. She was struggling to adjust to finding a new job and raising her two children alone. The juggling of housework, child-rearing, and being suddenly single was almost too much to bear at one time. She thought she was going to explode emotionally. "I'm close to a nervous breakdown," she wept. "I want the merry-go-round to stop."

Are Donna, Ralph, and Marcy crazy? Are they mentally ill? Do they have a disease or sickness? The answer is no. They are just ordinary people who have been exposed to some of the common difficulties of life. They are tired and hurting. They don't want to face any more conflict. They would like the pain to go away. They would like some peace in the midst of the storms of life.

It seems the term "mental illness" has become a catchall for any problem that overwhelms individuals or any behavior that society has a difficult time dealing with. The common word *crazy* also encompasses any difficulties from being overworked to bizarre behavior.

As one reads through history, it is easy to see that emotional problems, conflicts in relationships, and strange behaviors have been experienced by all generations. From earliest recorded history, there have been mentions of mental disturbances and emotional problems among people.

The Search for Understanding Life's Problems

Down through the years, philosophers, artists, clergymen, scientists, and physicians have endeavored to understand the nature of man. They have tried to understand his eternal fears and the motivation for his behavior. The approaches have basically fallen into three categories:

> 1. They have looked for external organic and physical causes for abnormal behavior. This has involved the biological and medical sciences.
>
> 2. They have attempted to discover internal psychological reasons for people's thoughts and actions. This has given rise to psychological studies and countless theories as to the motivation of human beings.
>
> 3. They have explained people's conduct by ways of the influence of the stars, demons, magic, or the gods. This viewpoint has resulted in fears, magical rituals, exorcism, incantations, intimidation, forced confessions, torture, and death.

The Babylonians and Egyptians practiced astrology and believed that the stars influenced human behavior. They used magical procedures to deal with strange conduct.

The Greeks believed that insanity came from the gods. It was also believed that the four body humors—

blood, phlegm, yellow bile, and black bile—determined how people acted. It was commonly thought that hysteria was caused by a wandering uterus, loosened from its moorings in the pelvic cavity. It was thought that only by intercourse and marriage could a cure for the condition be found.

The Arabs believed that the insane were somehow divinely inspired and not victims of demons. They built a number of asylums for those who were believed to be mentally sick.

In the 1300s and 1400s, witch-hunts arose in Europe. An antierotic movement was started. It was believed that witches (mostly women) were the stimuli for men's licentiousness. The general population thought that witches had the ability to change men into animals by use of magical arts. It was also believed that witches could destroy the ability of women to have children and could produce abortions. It was believed that diseases came from witchcraft, and plagues were the result of sins. People were burned at the stake for their socially unacceptable behavior.

In the past, men created witches:
now they create mental patients.
—Thomas Szasz

In 1547, the Bethlem Royal Hospital was founded in London, England. It was later transformed into a mental hospital. The name "Bethlem" was mispronounced by the common man and was vocalized as "Bedlam." The hospital soon became a curiosity for those in society. Visitors would come to watch the patients rage, scream, and babble incoherently. The inmates at "Bedlam" would laugh strangely, tear their clothing, and excrete anywhere. At the height of its operation, "Bedlam" entertained over 96,000 visitors a year. It became a human zoo.

During the 1700s and 1800s, asylums were used to house the insane, deformed, mentally retarded, and paupers. Often the asylums or "madhouses" would have as many as 300 to 500 patients at a time. The "lunatics" were confined in iron cages with chains and manacles. Rape and murder were commonplace in the asylums. Often records were forged to hide details of embezzlement of funds, unexplained deaths, and records of normal individuals who were forced into the asylums by relatives.

The "crazy" were exposed to utter filth and neglect. All forms of sickness were left untreated. Often the inmates were chained to walls and left naked. Some lost toes due to frostbite. Beatings, whippings, being locked into wooden cribs, and other forms of maltreatment occurred frequently. Maggots and various forms of insects were found in the food.

Bleeding of patients was a standard practice. Electric shock, drugs, and surgery were used on the "lunatics." The "mad" people were wrapped in cold sheets. The pain of this process was so intense that the prisoners would scream for hours. They would have ice-cold water thrown on them. Their muscles and joints would atrophy due to restraints and the lack of exercise.

A "spinning chair" was invented to calm those who were out of control. It was believed that congested blood in the brain led to mental illness. Doctors thought that this condition would be relieved by rotary motion. This chair would go round and round causing the patients to vomit and eventually become disoriented, and finally pass out.

The psychiatrist unfailingly recognizes
the madman by his excited behavior
on being incarcerated.
—Karl Kraus

In the mid-1800s reformers tried to change the conditions of the asylums. It is said that after entering the asylums, the reformers were almost overcome by the stench of body odor and excrement everywhere. The smell would remain in their clothes even after leaving the premises.

Individuals like Philippe Pinel, William Battie, John Conolly, Benjamin Rush, Thomas Kirkbride, Dorothea L. Dix, and William James deplored the treatment given at state hospitals. They believed benevolence and kindness were better cures. They strove to change the image of the "insane and mad." Over the years, their impact along with that of others has helped to change the brutality and harshness of asylums. Their influence caused a host of people to take a serious look at those who were suffering because of emotional problems. Many learned individuals began to spend their lives in search of answers for the human condition.

Here Come the Psychiatrists

Franz Anton Mesmer was born in 1734 and believed that the human body contained a magnetic fluid. He created a very popular method of treating illness by using magnets and hypnotism.

In 1791, Franz Joseph Gall developed a new "science" called phrenology. He believed that people's behaviors could be detected by the bumps on their heads. For example, if someone was filled with pride, the organ of self-esteem would be enlarged compared to other organs in the mind. That enlargement of the organ of self-esteem would cause a bump that could be felt by the doctor. Ernst Kretschmer, on the other hand, believed that an individual's body shape determined his or her actions. To prove his theory, he wrote a book entitled *Physique and Character*.

From the latter part of the 1800s to the present, there have been many notable individuals who have made contributions in the field called "psychiatry." Included are:

Jean-Martin Charcot	Wilhelm Griesinger
Otto Rank	Pierre Janet
Sigmund Freud	Karen Horney
A. A. Liebault	Alfred Adler
Harry Stack Sullivan	Hippolyte Bernheim
Wilhelm Stekel	Erich Fromm
Ivan P. Pavlov	Carl Jung
Sandor Rado	Adolf Meyer
Wilhelm Reich	Erick Erikson
Morton Prince	Melanie Klein
Joseph Wolpe	

At the present time, there are more than 300 schools of therapy, or psychological approaches for dealing with the emotional hurts and ills of people. One can become very confused by the many voices of those in psychological and counseling fields who contend that their approach is the best way.

---

*Man is certainly stark mad; he cannot
make a worm, and yet he will be
making gods by dozens.*
—Michel de Montaigne

It is amazing what human beings have done to other human beings. With little information we program and direct their lives, often in the name of science and concern for humanity. For the moment, let's pretend that you are a world-renowned psychiatrist. You have been trained in the best schools in the country. You have written books and lectured on mental illness. I now bring you three case studies for your diagnosis.

Case Study Number One

The first "patient" is a sixteen-year-old girl. She was orphaned and willed to the custody of her grandmother by her mother. The mother was separated from an alcoholic husband, who was now deceased. The mother rejected the homely girl. The child had been proven to steal sweets. At five years of age she swallowed a penny to attract attention. The father had been fond of the child. The young girl lived in fantasy as the mistress of her father's household for years. She has four young uncles and aunts living in the household. They cannot be managed by the grandmother, who is widowed. One young uncle drinks, has a love affair, and locks himself in a room. The grandmother resolves to be more strict with the children. She dresses the granddaughter oddly. She refuses to let the young girl have playmates. She put her in braces to keep her back straight. The grandmother did not send her to grade school. The aunt on the paternal side of the family is crippled and the uncle asthmatic. How will this young girl turn out?

Case Study Number Two

The second "patient" is a boy in his senior year of secondary school. He has obtained a certificate from a physician stating that a nervous breakdown makes it necessary for him to leave school for six months. The boy is not a good all-around student. He has no friends. The teachers find him a problem. He spoke late. His father is ashamed of his son's lack of athletic ability. He has very poor adjustment to school. The boy has mannerisms. He makes up his own religion and chants hymns to himself. His parents regard him as different. How will this young man turn out?

Case Study Number Three

The final "patient" is a six-year-old boy. He had a large head at birth. The doctors thought he might have had brain fever. Three of his siblings had died before his birth. His mother does not agree with the relatives and neighbors that the child is probably abnormal. The child is sent to school and diagnosed as mentally ill by the teacher. The mother is angry and withdraws him from school. She says that she will teach him herself. How will this young boy turn out?[1]

As the world-famous psychiatrist, you can now diagnose how these three young people will turn out in life. Use the chart below to rate the possible outcomes.

Possible Outcomes	Case #1	Case #2	Case #3
1. Will outgrow difficulties			
2. Will not outgrow difficulties without psychological or psychiatric help			
3. Will be mentally deficient			
4. Will be gifted			
5. Will be psychotic and need to be institutionalized			
6. Will be delinquent			
7. Will be neurotic, but otherwise will adjust to conditions without being institutionalized			
8. Other			

The above three children did grow up. They did make a contribution to society in spite of their negative environments. They did become productive, even though many said that they would never amount to anything. Case Study Number One was Eleanor Roosevelt. Case Study Number Two was Albert Einstein. Case Study Number Three was Thomas Alva Edison.

Have you grown up in a negative and maybe even hostile environment? Have other people told you that you would never amount to anything? Have you felt like the odds to succeed in life were against you? You are not alone.

Have you ever wondered if you were crazy? Have you thought that you might be moving in the direction of becoming crazy? To whom does one listen for advice? Whom can you trust to give you accurate feedback and direction for the problems that you face? How can you get help for your emotional difficulties if you don't live near a counselor? What are you to do if you cannot afford the high cost of counseling? Is it possible to become your own counselor?

It is my prayer that these questions will be answered as you begin to understand the concepts in this book. It is my conviction that many (if not most) individuals have within themselves great resources for solving their own problems and difficulties. With God's help and the use of the Bible, many problems will begin to resolve themselves, and for those that cannot be resolved, God will give the strength and grace to endure them. God will give you the ability to make peace with pain.

Do you want more and more of God's kindness and peace? Then learn to know him better and better. For as you know him better, he will give you, through his great power, everything you need for living a truly good life: he even shares his own glory and his own goodness with us!
(2 Peter 1:2,3).

CHAPTER TWO

A Fresh Look at Mental Illness

Take your life in your own hands, and what happens? A terrible thing: no one to blame.

—Erica Jong

Very few will forget the classic case of Dan White. His political dreams were dashed when San Francisco Mayor George Moscone and Supervisor Harvey Milk refused to reappoint White as a supervisor. White gained entrance to City Hall with a well-hidden gun and the intent to kill the men who destroyed his career. Somehow he got through the metal detectors, found the mayor in his office, and shot him five times. He then reloaded, sought out Harvey Milk, and shot him four times.

At Dan White's trial, his lawyers went for the insanity plea. The psychiatrists insisted that White was suffering from diminished capacity. The psychiatrists suggested that living at home and consuming Cokes, Twinkies, and other junk food caused White's diminished capacity. This was known as the "Twinkie Defense." You see, White was not responsible for his actions. He was mentally ill. It was the Twinkies that made him do it.[1]

When John W. Hinkley, Jr., shot President Ronald Reagan, the psychiatrists had a feeding frenzy. Hinkley was not responsible. He was not a criminal. He was a hapless victim of society. At the time, Harvard psychiatrist Thomas Gutheil suggested that Hinkley was a victim suffering from the disease of "erotomania." This is an illness caused by "the obsession with celebrities." Anyone who would want to kill the president of the United States had to be mentally ill. God forbid that Hinkley be classified as an evil or wicked man! He couldn't possibly be a self-motivated, attention-seeking murderer. No one would dare suggest that he was a terrorist. He was just a sick man.[2]

Though this be madness, yet
there is method in it.
—William Shakespeare

Our society is very degree-oriented. When people have an M.D. or a Ph.D. behind their name, we tend to set them apart as authorities or experts. We become captivated by their theories and academic background. When those with the degrees tell us we are mentally ill or have a mental illness, we believe them.

What If Mental Illness Doesn't Exist?

Mental illness is not truly an illness in the medical sense. It is simply a metaphor to describe behaviors in a person's life. When we say that someone is "lovesick," does he or she really have a physical disease? Of course not. It is just a metaphor to describe a feeling. It is not a true illness. We often use this type of language when describing troubled relationships between people. The phrase "You make me sick" is not describing a disease. "He is a real pain in the neck" is not a medical illness. It may be descriptive of a damaged relationship, but certainly not of an ailment.

But you might ask the question, "If there is not mental illness, then are the people well?" The answer is yes, they are well. "But they are not feeling good." True. They are not feeling good. They are unhappy. You see, it is possible to be well in the physical and medical sense and still be unhappy at the same time.

Psycho-Babble

I think herein lies the problem. Those in the medical and psychological fields have designed unhappiness as an illness. They have gone on to expand this even further by saying crime is an illness. Poverty is an illness. Overeating is an illness (bulimia). Undereating is an illness (anorexia nervosa). Overdrinking is an illness (alcoholism). Betting too much money is an illness (pathological gambling). Stealing things from stores is an illness (kleptomania). The fear of being in public places is an illness (agoraphobia).

If an individual does not pay attention, it is an illness (attention deficit disorder with hyperactivity). If someone sets buildings on fire, it is an illness (pyromania). If I'm a man and dress in women's clothes, it is an illness (transvestism). If I am selfish and filled with pride, it is an illness (narcissistic personality disorder). If I smoke too much, it is an illness (tobacco use disorder). If I have persistent thoughts and repetitive behaviors, it is an illness (obsessive compulsive disorder). If I have had a hurtful past experience, it is an illness (post-traumatic stress disorder).

Schizophrenia is the name for a condition that most psychiatrists ascribe to patients they call schizophrenic.
—*R. D. Laing*

Where does it all end? If I don't like school it is an illness (school phobia). If I have bad dreams, it is an illness (sleep terror disorder). If I sneak around people's houses and look in their windows, it is an illness (voyeurism). If I wear a trench coat with no clothes on, and then open the coat and show someone my naked body, or take down my pants and moon someone, it is an illness (exhibitionism). If I don't agree with someone's lifestyle of being a homosexual, it is an illness (homophobia). If I have an excessive enthusiasm for drinking water, it is an illness (psychogenic plydipsia).

Who Is Responsible?

This foolishness needs to stop. How long shall we go on describing socially unacceptable behavior as an illness? Is it really healthy to tell people that they are sick when they are simply exercising behaviors that either irritate themselves or annoy other people?

Is it not possible that what experts call "mental illness" is simply a conflict between what people do and what other people will accept? We cannot go on describing human problems as "illness." Social and moral disagreements are not diseases. Disagreements of a personal, legal, political, or religious nature are certainly not sicknesses in medical terms.

---

*We must remember that every "mental"
symptom is a veiled cry of anguish.
Against what? Against oppression, or
what the patient experiences as oppression.
The oppressed speak a million tongues.*
—Thomas Szasz

This does not in any way mean that there are not problems. Life is filled with personal misery. Social unrest has been part of the human condition since recorded history began. Suffering has been experienced by everyone at some time in life. So what else is new? Although these experiences are common, no matter the race or ethnic origin, they are not a disease. They are not an illness.

When we call unpleasantness, suffering, pain, or criminal behavior a disease, we rob ourselves of integrity. When we categorize negative individual actions as an illness, we erase individual responsibility and accountability. When we take away responsibility and accountability, we destroy hope of change.

To call wickedness or strange behavior an illness creates an excuse mechanism for it to continue. I am not the guilty or responsible party. It is the illness or disease *in* me that causes my weird actions. If only the disease would go away, then I wouldn't act the way I do. If I didn't have this illness, I wouldn't be the failure I am. Blame-shifting has become a way of life for many people.

A Rose Garden?

If I accept responsibility for my actions, will my life become a rose garden? Will I be happy all of the time? Will everything run smoothly for me? Will I escape the problems that other people face? Of course not.

Where is it written that anyone has a guarantee that life will be just one big, joyous party? All of human history and personal experience argue against that type of thinking.

It is from the struggles of life that a person becomes strong and mature. We admire those who have gone through tough times and have emerged victorious. We desire to have the strength of character these people display. The only problem is that we want the gain without the pain. We want the positive character traits without going through the fire of adversity.

Once I do away with the myth of mental illness, I immediately gain hope. I am responsible for most of the predicaments in which I find myself. There is a part I play in change. Once this realization comes to mind, I can then get on with the business of making positive changes in my life. I can learn how to face problems and difficulties. I can become the veteran of life who faces struggles with courage and a positive spirit.

How Can You Be So Brash?

I am sure there will be some readers who will say, "Now just a minute! Do you really mean that there is no such a thing as mental illness?"

In the true medical sense, there is no such thing as mental illness. The mind is the brain's thinking process. A thinking process cannot have a disease or become ill. If you were to do an autopsy on someone who had died and was said to have had a mental illness like multiple-personality disorder, would you find the disease? Would you find the microbe or virus of a personality disorder? You would not. The same is true of most of what is called mental illness.

Now granted, there are diseases of the brain such as cerebral syphilis; encephalitis; frontal lobe and temporal lobe tumors; cerebral arteriosclerosis, strokes, and embolisms; aphasia and apraxia; senile dementia, and Alzheimer's disease. These are true illnesses. There are chemical imbalances in the human body that directly influence the emotions and thinking process. Diabetes, hypoglycemia, thyroid imbalances, and estrogen deficiencies are a few examples. Birth defects, mental retardation, and accidents also affect the brain and the thinking process. All of the above are true diseases, illnesses, or physical defects. There is no argument over these types of afflictions. They are understandable and can be traced to their origin. They are diseases of the body and brain . . . but they are not mental illness.

There is no microorganism that enters my body, moves to the brain, and causes me to murder my spouse. I may be drunk, jealous, or enraged, but I am not ill.

There is no parasite that comes from outside and causes me to become a chronic liar or thief. These are chosen human behaviors that have nothing to do with disease.

Bacteria do not cause me to overeat or starve myself. A broken relationship or a low self-image may be the cause, but not some type of germ.

Viruses do not cause me to drink, use drugs, gamble, or take my clothes off in public places. These are behaviors of choice, not random illnesses that overtake my body.

Neurotics build castles in the air.
Psychotics live in the castles.
Psychiatrists collect the rent.

How is so-called "mental illness" dealt with today? How are the "diseases" of mental dysfunction cured? The most common approaches utilize drugs, electric shock, surgery, or therapy sessions.

Drugs do not cure negative thinking processes. Drugs only numb, slow, or dull thinking. Electric shock may frazzle the brain, but it is not a joyous event to which most people look forward. Brain surgery may erase memory and emotions; however, I don't think it could be classified as cosmetic or plastic surgery.

By far, the most common practice for dealing with mental and emotional problems is called "therapy." Therapy is where an individual discusses his problems with another person. Can you imagine that—a talking cure for a disease? I wish we could talk to cancer and make it go away. Wouldn't it be great if a group discussion could eliminate heart disease? Maybe if I would pound a pillow and scream, my gall bladder infection would disappear.

Please do not misunderstand. I am not suggesting that talking about problems and gaining insight is not beneficial. I am just attempting to point out that talking does not cure a disease. This is simply because there is no disease (in the true medical sense) in the first place.

We acknowledge that there are certain brain diseases, birth defects, and chemical imbalances. But these medical conditions do not affect the general population on a large scale. They affect a very small minority of the people in the world. The vast majority of people who encounter depression, anxiety, and other problems and difficulties are not ill. They are troubled and not feeling good emotionally, but they are not diseased or sick.

The majority of problems that are classified as some form of mental illness are in reality:

- broken relationships
- unfulfilled or unrealistic expectations of life
- guilt over not doing what we should do
- disobedience
- not accepting responsibility
- inability to adjust to and accept hurtful experiences
- unwillingness to let go of the past and forgive others
- low self-image or high, perfectionist standards

We must stop calling extreme wickedness "mental illness." We must put an end to telling people they are sick, when the truth is that they are just exercising behaviors with which they are not happy and that others get upset over. We need to realize that we may be holding unrealistic expectations about life and relationships with people.

It is not healthy for the individual (or society in general) to believe that he is just a victim with no control over his life or behavior. I think this type of advice robs the individual of integrity and self-respect. It creates a patient-and-doctor relationship. It encourages dependency and introversion.

Mental, emotional, and spiritual growth come from facing problems rather than running from them. It involves struggle, pain, and courage. It requires exercise of the will and the determination to not give up. Out of the battles and conflicts of life our spirit and character are molded. When we accept responsibility for our own actions and attitudes, we grow toward maturity. We gain self-respect and begin to adjust to the pain that is common to all people.

> Dear brothers, is your life full of difficulties and temptations? Then be happy, for when the way is rough, your patience has a chance to grow. So let it grow, and don't try to squirm out of your problems. For when your patience is finally in full bloom, then you will be ready for anything, strong in character, full and complete (James 1:2-4).

CHAPTER THREE

A World Gone Mad

This tendency to avoid problems and the emotional suffering inherent in them is the primary basis of all human mental illness.

—M. Scott Peck

In the first two chapters, we have suggested that life is filled with pain and suffering. Physical, mental, emotional, social, and spiritual problems are part of the human experience. No one likes to hurt. No one seeks misery as a way of life. It is how we face our problems that determines our peace. It is our attitude that brings joy and contentment.

Often people run from their problems. They try to deny their difficulties. Some will go to great lengths to escape from suffering. They will do almost anything rather than experience pain or the struggle that comes from solving problems.

Rather than growing through the unpleasant experiences of life, some people will develop what is called "neurosis." "Neurosis" refers to any type of disorder of the mind or emotion that is without obvious organic cause. It could include anxiety, phobias, obsessive-compulsive thoughts or actions, hypochondria, or other abnormal behavior.

When neurotic behavior does not lessen the pain, pressure, or stress of uncomfortable situations, individuals may go on to develop what is called "psychosis." This involves severe mental disorders characterized by the inability to function on a "normal" level of intellectual or social interaction. Sometimes people who display this type of behavior will retreat or withdraw from reality. They begin to live in a fantasy world of their own creation.

The neurotic assumes too much responsibility;
the person with a character disorder
not enough.
—M. Scott Peck

Carl Gustav Jung was a contemporary of Sigmund Freud. He, along with Freud, was a very famous psychotherapist. In his book *Memories, Dreams, Reflections*, he tells a most interesting story from his childhood about neurosis:

> One day in the early summer of 1887 I was standing in the cathedral square, waiting for a classmate who went home by the same route as myself. It was twelve o'clock, and the morning classes were over. Suddenly another boy gave me a shove that knocked me off my feet. I fell, striking my head against the curbstone so hard that I almost lost consciousness. For about half an hour afterward I was a little dazed. At the moment I felt the blow the thought flashed through my

mind: "Now you won't have to go to school anymore." I was only half unconscious, but I
remained lying there a few moments longer than
was strictly necessary, chiefly in order to avenge
myself on the assailant. Then people picked me
up and took me to a house nearby, where two
elderly spinster aunts lived. From then on I
began to have fainting spells whenever I had to
return to school, and whenever my parents set
me to doing my homework. For more than six
months I stayed away from school, and for me
that was a picnic. I was free, could dream for
hours, be anywhere I liked, in the woods or by
the water, or draw.[1]

Every now and then, Jung would have flashes of
reality and the awareness that his actions were not
bringing satisfaction. In his inmost being he knew that
his behaviors were dishonest.

But I was growing more and more away from
the world, and had all the while faint pangs of
conscience. I frittered away my time with loafing,
collecting, reading, and playing. But I did not feel
any happier for it; I had the obscure feeling that I
was fleeing from myself.[2]

Toward the end of Jung's six months of loafing, a
shocking event happened to him. He was confronted
with the cause-and-effect relationship of his actions.
He was forced to take responsibility for what he was
doing.

Then one day a friend called on my father.
They were sitting in the garden and I hid behind

a shrub, for I was possessed of an insatiable curiosity. I heard the visitor saying to my father, "And how is your son?" "Ah, that's a sad business," my father replied. "The doctors no longer know what is wrong with him. They think it may be epilepsy. It would be dreadful if he were incurable. I have lost what little I had, and what will become of the boy if he cannot earn his own living?"

I was thunderstruck. This was a collision with reality. "Why, then, I must get to work!" I thought suddenly.

From that moment on I became a serious child. I crept away, went to my father's study, took out my Latin grammar, and began to cram with intense concentration. After ten minutes of this I had the finest of fainting fits. I almost fell off the chair, but after a few minutes I felt better and went on working. "Devil take it, I'm not going to faint," I told myself, and persisted in my purpose. This time it took about fifteen minutes before the second attack came. That, too, passed like the first. "And now you must really get to work!" I stuck it out, and after an hour came the third attack. Still I did not give up, and worked for another hour, until I had the feeling that I had overcome the attacks. Suddenly I felt better than I had in all the months before. And in fact the attacks did not recur. From that day on I worked over my grammar and other schoolbooks every day. A few weeks later I returned to school, and never suffered another attack, even there. The whole bag of tricks was over and done with! That was when I learned what neurosis is.[3]

*Neurosis is always a substitute
for legitimate suffering.*
—Carl Jung

*Schizophrenic behaviour is a special strategy
that a person invents in order to live
in an unlivable situation.*
—R. D. Laing

It is only when people hurt enough that they begin to work on their problems. Take, for example, the familiar story of the prodigal son found in Luke chapter 15 in the Bible. As you recall, a certain man had two sons. The younger son was tired of living at home and wanted to strike out on his own. He wanted to escape from the restraints of his family. He asked his father for his share of his inheritance. The father gave it to the boy. The young man spent all of his money in loose living and having a good time. When he finally spent all of his money, he had to go to work feeding slop to the pigs.

It was in the pigpen that the young man came to his senses. He began to realize how good he had had it back at home. He then returned to his father to ask forgiveness and to be restored. His father received his son with open arms.

Have you ever wondered what would have happened if the young man had returned home before he had reached the pain of the pigpen? He would have left home again. People have to come to the end of themselves . . . they have to hurt enough to change. Have you made it to the pigpen yet? Are you hurting enough to change?

There are many schools of thought on how to deal with the problems and difficulties of life. Let's for a moment take a look at a few of the more popular models for dealing with the human condition.

We will use the analogy of a man who has a great deal of pain in his life because of his continual sitting on a tack. He is tired of the pain and goes to a counselor for relief.

The first counselor he visits is a follower of Carl Rogers who established Client-Centered Therapy. The

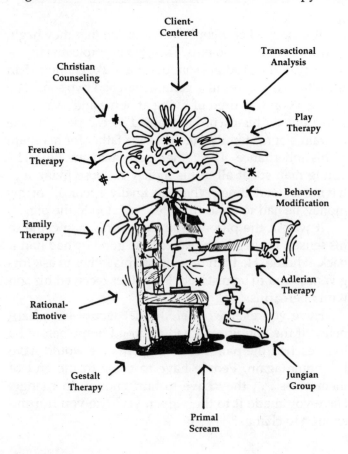

counselor says, "Talk to me about the problem that you are experiencing. The answer lies within you, and by using the talking process it will come to resolve itself."

He then goes to a counselor who emulates Eric Berne's Transactional Analysis. He is told to stop playing games. "Your screaming about the pain is very 'childish.' You need to ignore the 'parent' messages from your mind and begin to respond with maturity as an 'adult.' You need to rewrite the 'script' of your life."

Still experiencing pain, he drops in to see a disciple of Anna Freud who uses Play Therapy. Upon entering he is told, "Here are some dolls and a thumbtack. Would you please use them and show me what is happening to you?"

That was fun, but it did not resolve the issue. His next stop was at the B. F. Skinner Behavior Modification Institute. The doctor in charge began to poke him with a cattle prod each time he mentioned his pain. When he finally stopped talking about the pain, he was given some candy for his good behavior.

He walked out of the Behavior Institute with an extra bag of candy. That gave him enough energy to go across town to the Adlerian Therapy Center. Alfred Adler was not in, but a therapist was available to help him. After listening to his story, the therapist replied, "I can see that your whole body is involved with your pain. There must be a significant goal or purpose for all of your behavior."

Leaving a little confused, he walked down the block to the Jungian group therapy session that was being held in the local park. The entire group smiled as he sat down. The leader said, "Please share your thoughts with the entire group. They will help you work through your pain."

He had a nice time meeting new people, but still had this continual pain that he could not get rid of. As he walked by an open door, he heard a scream that startled him. Being curious, he entered and found himself in the middle of Arthur Janov's Primal Scream therapy session. He was told to grab a pillow and go to the center of the room. He was instructed to close his eyes and try and reexperience a childhood of hurt that is causing his pain today. "Let your hurt and pain out. . . . Scream about all the pain. Strike your pillow." That experience did let off some steam. It did feel good to strike the pillow and yell, but soon the pain returned.

A friend suggested that he visit the local Fritz Pearl's Gestalt therapist. After the normal chitchat introduction, the therapist suggested, "Let's bring your pain into the here and now. Use your imagination and place your pain in this empty chair. Now talk to your pain and let it know how you feel about it. Next, switch places with your pain. You become your pain and talk back to yourself." He soon left talking to himself and to the telephone pole outside.

He then picked up a book on Rational-Emotive Therapy by Albert Ellis. He learned that he had faulty thinking about his pain. He was letting his emotions control him. He realized that he needed to change his negative belief system.

For the next week, he kept telling himself that he had no pain. He tried to think only positive thoughts, especially after hearing a sermon on positive thinking by Norman Vincent Peale.

In the continuing search for relief, he visited a Family Therapist who was well-versed in Family Theory as taught by Bowen, Minuchin, and Watzlawick. "We need to look at your family system and network and see how it is influencing your present pain," said the family counselor.

This new information about his family led him to read some books on family interaction. He soon discovered that he was dysfunctional and very co-dependent. He was told that he was a victim of child abuse, and had most likely suffered emotional, physical, and sexual abuse that he had denied for years. He was told to discover the hidden child of his past and dredge up memories of past hurts and have them healed. This was a good experience because it gave him a great opportunity to talk about himself and tell everyone he knew that he was mad at his parents.

Child abuse may haunt the unconscious. . . .
It sometimes makes amnesiacs of its victims . . .
a paranoiac's delight. To be a victim you
don't have to remember your abuse,
you only need to imagine it.
—Wendy Kaminer

This proved to be a relief because he was tired of talking about job stress, family burnout, and the mid-life crisis he had been going through. This also gave him the opportunity to join a twelve-step program in the recovery movement and become a support-group junkie. He joined Alcoholics Anonymous, Adult Children of Alcoholics, Overeaters Anonymous, Narcotics Anonymous, Sex and Love Addicts, Reverse Discrimination Anonymous, and Adult Children of Tack Sitters Anonymous. He was joined by many others who loved to share their stories of pain and woe. He had the joy of experiencing "grief work." He was able to rid himself of "negative messages" and become less "toxic." But somehow he still had a great pain that lingered with him.

As a last resort he went in for some Freudian Psychoanalytic Therapy. He was told, "Your pain is near your sexual organs. You have a sexual problem."

It was only after some weeks that he ran into a Christian friend who said, "It sounds like you are in a lot of pain. Your pain would go away if you got up off the tack. I'll be glad to help you learn how to not sit on tacks in the future."

But You Don't Understand

"I think that you are making fun of the field of psychology. Psychologists and psychiatrists have made great contributions. You are oversimplifying the problems."

What I am suggesting is that problems and difficulties may not be as complex as most people think. You must realize, however, that there is a difference between simple and easy. I think there are a host of simple answers for most human problems. Truth is not complex. It is very plain. Applying the truth to everyday life, on the other hand, may be very difficult. For example, I may know the truth that smoking and alcohol are not good for my body. But to stop smoking or drinking may be an absolute battle in my life. I may know that I need to study for a test in order to pass it, but my whole emotional system may rebel against what I know I should be doing.

When it comes to the various approaches in the field of psychology, truth may be present alongside error. A particular method for dealing with emotional problems may have elements of truth in it. That is what makes it attractive and sometimes effective. It has been said that error always rides the back of truth.

ERROR ALWAYS RIDES THE BACK OF TRUTH!

Psycho-gate

Although I have studied in the field of psychology and counseling and am a licensed counselor, I have a very difficult time pointing to truly successful methods of counseling apart from the use of the Bible.

Even those in the secular field of psychology cannot point to success. The classic study by Hans J. Eysenck drives home this point. Dr. Eysenck was a psychologist at the British Institute of Psychiatry who wrote over 800 articles for scientific magazines and was the author of 30 books in the field of psychology. He investigated over 170 other studies on the effects of psychotherapy, and his findings were overwhelming.

The psychiatric community has to deal with the results.

Dr. Eysenck discovered that 44 percent of people who went for psychoanalytic therapy improved within two years. He also found that 64 percent of those who received eclectic therapy (various different approaches) improved within two years. The big shock was when he discovered that 72 percent of those who received no therapy improved within two years. To make matters worse, in a five-year follow-up, 90 percent of those who received no therapy improved.[4]

In his book *The Effects of Psychotherapy*, Dr. Eysenck says,

> Perhaps we may quote just two experienced psychoanalysts who have long spoken up in favor of Freudian theories. The first is D. H. Malan, Senior Hospital Medical Officer at the Tavistock Clinic in London. This is the strong point of orthodox psychoanalysis in England. Malan (1963) says, "There is not the slightest indication from the published figures that psychotherapy has any value at all" (p. 164). And in his recent book *Crisis in Psychiatry and Religion*, O. H. Mowrer, a former president of the American Psychological Association and for over thirty years a leading psychoanalyst and psychotherapist, has this to say: "From testimony now available from both the friends and foes of analysis it is clear that, at best, analysis casts a spell but does not cure" (p. 121). ". . . As a result of a succession of personal and professional experiences, I have become increasingly convinced, during the last ten or fifteen years, of the basic unsoundness of Freud's major premises" (p. 123). ". . . Psychiatrists and psychologists are rather generally abandoning

psychoanalytic theory and practice" (p. 134). ". . . There is not a shred of evidence that psychoanalyzed individuals permanently benefit from the experience, and there are equally clear indications that psychoanalysis, as a common philosophy of life, is not only nontherapeutic but actively pernicious" (p. 161).[5]

One of the striking differences between a cat and a lie is that a cat has only nine lives.
—Mark Twain

You may recall the classic experiment by Dr. D. L. Rosenhan. He was a professor of psychology and law at Stanford University. He and seven other perfectly sane individuals had themselves admitted to 12 different mental hospitals. Their plan was to tell one lie, and thereafter tell nothing but the truth. The lie they told the attending psychiatrists was that they (the patients) "were hearing voices." The results of the experiment would be comical if they weren't so sad.

Otherwise, these normal people, mostly graduate students, gave truthful histories to the psychiatrists. They were all diagnosed as "schizophrenic," except one who was diagnosed as "Manic-depressive." Once admitted, they acted perfectly normally; yet were held for 7 to 52 days (the average was 19) and were given over 2,100 pills total. The true patients on the wards often recognized them as pseudopatients but the staff never did. Once labeled, the staff's perception of them was apparently so profoundly colored that normal behavior was seen as part of their psychosis.

In an even more damning postscript to the experiment, Rosenhan told one hospital what he had done. He then told them that he would try to gain admission for another pseudopatient there within the next 3 months. Ever watchful for the pseudopatient who was never sent, the staff labeled 41 of the next 193 admissions as suspected pseudopatients; over half of these were so labeled by a psychiatrist. The experimenter concluded: "Any diagnostic process that lends itself so readily to massive errors of this sort cannot be a very reliable one."[6]

There have been a host of other studies on the effects of psychotherapy that come to the same conclusion. There have also been studies as to the effectiveness of lay helpers compared to professionals.

In 1979, Durlak, at the University of Southern Illinois, reviewed no less than forty-two studies that had compared the effectiveness of professional as against paraprofessional "helpers." He was able to reach the following conclusions: ". . . Findings have been consistent and provocative. Paraprofessionals achieve clinical outcomes equal to or significantly better than those obtained by professionals. . . . Moreover, professional mental health education, training and experience do not appear to be necessary prerequisites for an effective helping person."[7]

Regardless the emotional reaction I may receive from some of my fellow counselors, I am suggesting that people might do fine without us. Especially in light of the fact that "the suicide rate is significantly higher among psychiatrists than among those of any of the other sixteen specialty groups listed by the American Medical Association as a part of the medical profession."[8]

If all of this is true, our next-door neighbor or a close Chrisitan friend will most likely be as effective as a professional counselor in helping you to face the difficulties of life—and cheaper. Your minister will probably be more beneficial to you than someone trained solely as a therapist.

In the following chapters we will begin to look at the simplicity of truth. We will also examine how to apply the Bible to everyday problems and explore the possibility of becoming your own counselor.

> We can rejoice, too, when we run into problems and trials for we know that they are good for us—they help us learn to be patient. And patience develops strength of character in us and helps us trust God more each time we use it until finally our hope and faith are strong and steady. Then, when that happens, we are able to hold our heads high no matter what happens and know that all is well, for we know how dearly God loves us, and we feel this warm love everywhere within us because God has given us the Holy Spirit to fill our hearts with his love (Romans 5:3-5).

CHAPTER FOUR

Dealing with Depression

The most important thought I ever had was
that of my individual responsibility to God.

—*Daniel Webster*

In talking with our family doctor (who won the California Doctor of the Year Award), he shared that the largest single problem he treats is depression. It has been called the "common cold" of mental health. Many famous people have had bouts with depression. Winston Churchill struggled with it. The great preacher Charles Haddon Spurgeon battled depression for years. Abraham Lincoln said:

> I am now the most miserable man living. If what I feel were equally distributed to the whole human family, there would not be a cheerful face on the earth. Whether I shall ever be better, I cannot tell; I awfully forebode I shall not. To remain as I am is impossible. I must die or be better, it appears to me.

A Spiritual Virus

"Bob, I just don't care anymore. I'm tired and can't handle the pressure. I hurt too much."

I was in my office preparing for my day of counseling when Melody called. Her voice was very soft. I could hardly understand what she was saying. As she kept talking, I could tell that her speech was slow and slurred. I knew something was wrong.

I asked Melody if she had taken any pills. She hesitated and then said yes and that "It didn't matter anymore."

As I talked to Melody, I was snapping my fingers to get the attention of another counselor whose door happened to be open. I waved for him to come into the room. While she continued to talk, I wrote a note for him to call the emergency rescue team and send them to her house. I kept talking with Melody until she could no longer pronounce words. She hung up.

When I reached her home, the rescue team was bringing her out the door on a stretcher. They immediately took her to the emergency room of the hospital and pumped her stomach. She survived her attempted suicide.

You see, Melody had fallen in love with a young man who had gotten her pregnant. He proceeded to leave her for another woman. In her depression, she had an abortion. After the termination of the baby, she could not deal with the loss of her lover and the guilt of the abortion. She decided to escape from all her pain.

Where does so-called "mental illness" come from? How does it get started? Can I stop it from overtaking me? How do I deal with it when I get twisted in my thinking and overwhelmed by my emotions. How can I maintain good mental health?

It is always good to check into your physical health as a starting point. Is there some organic or biological reason for the way you are feeling? As was mentioned earlier, physical maladies are not usually the cause for most emotional upsets, but it is good to eliminate that possibility.

I believe the root cause for most difficulties encountered by the average person can be found in what the Bible calls the sin nature. When sin entered the human race, it caused an infection to spread to all mankind. This was not a physical infection. It was a spiritual and moral infection. The "sin virus" infected the thinking process of everyone.

Contrary to common belief today, men and women are not basically good and occasionally go bad. They are basically bad and occasionally become good. There is, in fact, a real battle between good and evil in this world system. We see this every day in the newspaper or on television. Denying this concept is like burying one's head in the sand.

To use a computer analogy, everyone who is born into this world is born with a defective chip. This chip infects the life with a moral virus that is selfish and self-centered. Consequently, human behavior often displays itself in negative and even hostile ways.

The sin virus entered the human race when Adam and Eve disobeyed God in the Garden of Eden. As a result of their sin, men and women were separated from God, and Adam and Eve tried to hide from His presence:

> And they heard the sound of the LORD God walking in the garden in the cool of the day, and the man and his wife hid themselves from the presence of the LORD God among the trees of the garden (Genesis 3:8 NASB).

Much of what is called mental illness involves a hiding from God, a hiding from others, and a hiding from ourselves. The hiding is coupled with guilt and shame, symbolized by Adam and Eve realizing that they were naked. This hiding is soon followed by blame-shifting and a refusal to accept responsibility for our own actions:

> And the man said, "The woman whom Thou gavest to be with me, she gave me from the tree, and I ate." And the woman said, "The serpent deceived me, and I ate" (Genesis 3:12,13 NASB).

Their sinfulness caused them to be cast out of the Garden. Mankind left the presence of God and began to wander in alienation and separation from Him. Men and women still refuse to follow God's plan for their lives and thus begin to wander both intellectually and emotionally.

After Adam and Eve left the Garden of Eden, Eve gave birth to Cain and then to Abel. It was in the life of Cain that we first see that the "sin virus" was passed on. As you study the life of Cain, you can see in microcosm the seeds of what is called "mental illness."

> Now the man had relations with his wife Eve, and she conceived and gave birth to Cain, and she said, "I have gotten a manchild with the help of the LORD" (Genesis 4:1 NASB).

In this verse life seems very normal. A man and wife have physical relations and produce a son. The name "Cain" means "to fashion or to shape a creature."

> And again, she gave birth to his brother
> Abel. And Abel was a keeper of flocks, but Cain
> was a tiller of the ground (Genesis 4:2 NASB).

The name "Abel" means "breath" or "vapor." Little did Adam and Eve know that Abel's name would signify the brevity of human life.

> So it came about in the course of time
> that Cain brought an offering to the LORD of
> the fruit of the ground (Genesis 4:3 NASB).

Evidently years pass, and we find Cain merely discharging a religious duty. The word for "Lord" is the Hebrew word *Yahweh*.

> And Abel, on his part also brought of the
> firstlings of his flock and of their fat portions.
> And the LORD had regard for Abel and his
> offering (Genesis 4:4 NASB).

Abel is found bringing the Lord the best of his flock (firstlings) and the best portion of the offering (the fat). In Leviticus 3:16 we are told that all of the fat portions belong to the Lord. Abel's offering and attitude seems to be motivated by love and faith rather than out of duty.

> But for Cain and for his offering He had
> no regard. So Cain became very angry and his
> countenance fell (Genesis 4:5 NASB).

Many scholars have theorized as to why God received Abel's offering and not Cain's. I personally believe that Cain was aware of the fact that God slew animals and covered Adam and Eve's nakedness. I believe that they passed this story on to their children. This was symbolic of the shedding of blood for the covering of sins. Hebrews 9:22 (NIV) states, "Without the shedding of blood there is no forgiveness." Cain's offering did not meet the standard of what God was requiring. If the proper offering would have been given by Cain, God would have received it.

Cain's anger arose out of jealousy and envy toward his brother Abel. His nonverbal body language gave away what he was feeling, and his countenance fell. In this verse we have a classic description of depression.

When individuals encounter a buildup of stress, it often leads to depression. As depression is prolonged, or is deepened, some people give way under the emotional load. They eventually take their own life as an escape from the hurt and pain they feel. Suicide is among the top ten causes of death in the United States. It is estimated that over 1000 people a day around the world take their own life.

Characteristics of Depression

> The spirit of a man can endure his sickness, but a broken spirit who can bear? (Proverbs 18:14 NASB).

Someone has said that a bad day is when you are driving down the freeway behind a group of Hell's Angels motorcycle riders and your horn sticks. Well, depression is more than a bad day. It is a state of unhappiness.

Depression carries a sense of hopelessness. There seems to be no way out of the difficulties you face. This despair gives rise to a loss of perspective, feelings of apathy, and the desire to withdraw from people and from life in general.

The psalmist describes depression with the following words:

> Now hear my prayers; oh, listen to my cry, for my life is full of troubles, and death draws near. They say my life is ebbing out—a hopeless case (Psalm 88:2-4).

> Save me, O my God. The floods have risen. Deeper and deeper I sink in the mire; the waters rise around me. I have wept until I am exhausted; my throat is dry and hoarse; my eyes are swollen with weeping, waiting for my God to act. I cannot even count all those who hate me without cause (Psalm 69:1-4).

> Listen to my prayer, O God; don't hide yourself when I cry to you. Hear me, Lord! Listen to me! For I groan and weep beneath my burden of woe. . . . My heart is in anguish within me. Stark fear overpowers me. Trembling and horror overwhelm me. Oh, for wings like a dove, to fly away and rest! I would fly to the far-off deserts and stay there. I would flee to some refuge from all this storm (Psalm 55:1,2,4-8).

With depression comes oversensitivity. The individual misinterprets the motivations of others and thinks that people are out to do him harm. Depressed people often lose their self-esteem and become hurt and angry. They cover a host of emotions with the great masquerade of depression.

*We would worry less about what others
think of us, if we realized
how seldom they do.*

Depression is not a cause. It is a result. Some situation or some individual brings about depression. It is not a disease or a disorder of the brain. It is the result of how we view life. It is a way of thinking and behaving.

It has been my experience that most people know when they are in trouble emotionally. They know that they are unhappy and would like to change. The first step for true change comes when you take ownership of your feelings and behavior. Hope comes when you take responsibility for your thinking and actions.

Causes of Depression

Depression can arise from one event in your life or from a host of events. More often than not, depression involves a buildup of problems and difficulties. For example, if you suddenly got a phone call that a loved one has been killed in an auto accident, you would be shocked. The shock would give way to denial or disbelief. This would give rise to anger over the hurt and loss. Since the loved one cannot be brought to life again, you may hold in the anger until it turns to a state of depression.

On the other hand, it may take more than one single event to bring about depression. If you lose your job, you may pull yourself together and seek another position without the experience of depression. But if you lose your job, your spouse gets sick, your house burns down, and people talk behind your back, the resulting buildup of problems might bring about a state of depression. For many people, the deep wounds they experience over a period of time help them to form depression as a lifestyle.

The causes of depression fall into four basic categories: situational, physical, psychological, and spiritual. Situations that could bring about depression would be things like a great deal of stress over a period of time. It could include the loss of a job, loss of a relationship, or the loss of a home through fire or flood. The death of a loved one would come under this category.

Physical causes for depression could include sleep loss and sickness. Improper diet and not eating regularly could help to bring about depression. A reaction to drugs or alcohol could trigger it. Biological changes or chemical imbalance within your body could be a factor. Let me pause here to say that when you have experienced depression for an extended period of time, it may be wise to have a physical examination taken as a precaution. I also want to be very straightforward and say that it is very rare that biological changes or chemical imbalance are the causes of depression. Most depression arises out of broken relationships and conflict between people.

In the area of psychological causes for depression, this could include a negative self-image and self-pity. Faulty reasoning and the inability to process facts could lead to depressive thoughts. Conflict with people is probably the largest single contributor to depression. Often when in conflict with someone, we replay the conflict over and over in our minds. We carry on imaginary conversations with the person or persons we have difficulty with. We often can't or won't let go of the problem until we are completely worn out and mentally exhausted from rehearsing the discord.

Spiritual causes for depression could be brought about by feelings of emptiness and meaninglessness. We may feel that we are alienated from God. We may feel like there is a vacuum in life that needs to be filled. There also may be true guilt that we are facing. We may have done something wrong or said something wrong. Repentance or restoration may need to take place, and the longer we wait to do what we know needs to be done, the deeper the depression grows.

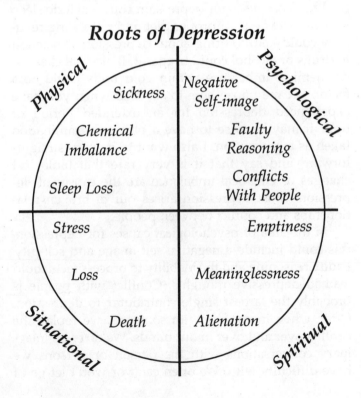

Roots of Depression

Physical

Sickness

Chemical Imbalance

Sleep Loss

Psychological

Negative Self-image

Faulty Reasoning

Conflicts With People

Situational

Stress

Loss

Death

Spiritual

Emptiness

Meaninglessness

Alienation

The Desire to Die

The story of Elijah the prophet has often been used as an illustration of someone going through depression. This story is found in the book of 1 Kings chapters 18 and 19. I would like you to look with new eyes at a very familiar story.

You will recall that Elijah meets King Ahab on the top of Mount Carmel for a showdown. Ahab brings 450 prophets of Baal and 400 prophets of Asherah who are Queen Jezebel's special prophets. Also in attendance are the Children of Israel.

Elijah challenges everyone there to choose to follow Baal or to follow God. Both sides build altars and agree that if Baal brings fire out of the sky to light the altar that the people will follow Baal, and if God sends fire to light the altar that the people will follow God. As you remember, God and not Baal sends fire from the sky. The prophets of Baal and Asherah are slain, and the people agree to follow God.

The next day Jezebel sends a message to Elijah that she is going to have him killed. He runs for his life. He goes into the wilderness and wants to die. He says, "It is enough; now, O Lord, take my life, for I am not better than my fathers." Elijah is in deep depression.

You have probably heard sermons in which it was suggested that every emotional high or successful endeavor is followed by depression, and that Elijah just needed rest and some food. I would like to suggest that there may be more to the picture than those concepts.

It has been my experience that after a success there may be a small downside. But it doesn't drop very far—not far enough to lead to depression. After emotional highs or successful endeavors, the downside that is experienced only lasts until the individual finds another goal to pursue. Success does not drain motivation. It usually increases it.

In the case of Elijah, I think his depression was the result of great pressures over a long period of time. It was not the result of one conflict on Mount Carmel. Jezebel's comments were only "the final straw that broke the camel's back."

Three-and-a-half years earlier, Elijah prayed that there would be no rain on the land because of the sin of the people. As a result of his prayer, no rain came and the crops died. With no crops came famine and cannibalism. Who did the people blame for all their suffering? You guessed it—Elijah. They wanted to kill him. He had to hide. After his confrontation on Mount Carmel, Jezebel said that he would be killed like her prophets.

Let's look at the buildup:

1. Three-and-a-half years of running and hiding (a very lonely time with loss of relationships).

2. Nobody liked him. His reputation was destroyed.

3. The emotional face-off with Ahab, the prophets, and the Children of Israel. Elijah was on one side and everyone else was on the other side. Elijah stood alone against the crowd.

4. Elijah slays the prophets (no small emotional trauma).

5. He runs over 20 miles back to the city (great fatigue).

6. He hears that Jezebel wants to kill him. "What's the use?" thoughts entered his mind.

7. He had emotions of frustration and anger.

8. He had emotions of self-pity.

My guess is that Elijah had come to the end of his string. It did not just happen in one day. He was emotionally and physically tired. He was spiritually down. He was angry and felt great waves of self-pity.

> I have been very zealous for the LORD, the God of hosts [great emotional and physical energy]; for the sons of Israel have forsaken Thy covenant, torn down Thine altars and killed Thy prophets with the sword [great anger]. And I alone am left [loneliness]; and they seek my life, to take it away [self-pity] (1 Kings 19:10 NASB).

Have you had a long buildup of problems and difficulties? Are you feeling tired and alone? Are you angry at the unfairness and injustice you face? Have you experienced loss, broken relationships, and unresolved conflict with others? Are you feeling a little sorry for yourself? Are you feeling depressed? Has it been going on for a long period of time? Would you like a way out? Would you like some relief?

Climbing Out of the Pit

The first step to getting out of the pit of despair is to realize that you are in the pit. The second step is to ask, "Do I want to get out?" "That's a stupid question," you say. Not really. Some people like the pit. Some people enjoy the pain. Some people get attention when they are in the pit. They would rather have the attention than relief from their misery.

Sometimes people are not totally clear about their depression. They are not aware of the hold it has on them. Let's get some clarity.

The Pit of Despair

	Mental	Physical	Emotional	Spiritual	
Mild Depression (Hours/Days) Normal Functioning	Self-doubt Resentment Self-pity	Loss of appetite Sleeplessness Unkempt appearance	Discontent Sadness Irritability	Question God's will Displeased with God's will Ungrateful Unbelieving	**Discouraged** People usually try to handle the problem alone.
Moderate Depression (Weeks) Impaired Functioning	Self-critical Anger Self-pity	Apathy Hypochondria "Weeps"	Distress Sorrow Loneliness	Anger at God's will Rejects God's will Gripes about God's will	**Despondent** People often talk with others to get advice and help with problem.
Severe Depression (Months/Years) Incapacitated Functioning	Self-rejection Bitterness Self-pity	Withdrawal Passivity Catatonia	Hopelessness Schizophrenia Abandonment	Resentment of God's Word Indifferent to God's Word Unbelief in God's Word	**Despair** People move from talking about the problem to taking drugs and electric shock treatment.

Suicide: 180° Murder

What is your sleep pattern like? Is it restful or restless? Do you sleep a normal amount of time, or do you only get a small amount of sleep? Your sleep pattern is one of the best gauges to tell if you are depressed or not. If you have little sleep, restless sleep, or too much sleep, you are most likely depressed about something.

Next I would like to suggest an unpleasant thought. It is possible to be angry without being depressed, but almost impossible to be depressed without being angry. *angry* What are you angry about? Is it a hurt or a loss? Who are you angry with? Are you mad with yourself, or mad at God? Are you angry with some family member, friend, or your boss? Are you angry about some situation in which you find yourself? You must deal with anger to deal with depression. Some people would rather be depressed than deal with their hurt and anger.

If I were personally talking with you I would ask, "How long have you felt sad (or depressed)?" As soon as you would tell me how long, I would ask, "What event in your life happened at that time? What events have reinforced this feeling since that time?"

Major Factors in Depression:
1. Hurt
2. Anger
3. Loss
4. Loneliness
5. Guilt

Let's say that you are feeling depressed and want to be your own counselor. One way to find out what is depressing you, if you're not sure, is to reverse your day. Don't start at the beginning of your day. Start at the end.

For example, let's say that it is 10:00 P.M. and you are about ready to go to bed. You have been feeling sad. You have no energy to do normal tasks. You have had a down feeling all day. You have the "blahs." Suddenly, it enters your head that you are feeling depressed. You begin to reverse your day.

You say to yourself, "It's 10:00 P.M. Nothing unusual happened between 10:00 P.M. and dinner." You go back further in your day. "I was on the freeway coming home and nothing happened but that crazy driver. That's not enough to depress me." You continue. "I was in the office writing letters. Nothing there to bother me. Before that, my secretary came in and talked to me and gave me some messages. No, that didn't bother me. I had several phone calls before lunch. No, not there. I had lunch with Stan. That was a good time. Before lunch Mike called. Bingo! That's it. That conversation would be enough to depress any-one! The nerve of Mike to say what he said. We really had a blowout over the phone."

Usually a certain conversation or event triggers depressive thoughts. Depressive thoughts are filled with hurt, loss, guilt, and anger. When the thoughts are not worked through, dealt with, and reconciled, they can cause strong mood changes which can lead to depression.

You may have to go back further than a day. For example, some people have down feelings at certain times of the year. I remember for a number of years that I would feel down in October and in the latter part of January. It took me several years before I noticed that there was a pattern. When I realized that there was a pattern, I asked myself, "What happened in October and the latter part of January?" As I reviewed my life, I realized that I had had some very hurtful experiences during those times of the year.

Something had triggered my memory of those events. It is sort of a déjà vu experience. You feel like you have got that "I have been here before," or "This has happened before" feeling. What brings that about? It could be a number of things hidden in the memory banks. It might have been the same weather conditions. It might have been the smell of orange blossoms that were present in October. You might have driven by some restaurant or neighborhood where the negative event took place. Something triggers the recollection of a past negative experience. It briefly comes to mind and then leaves, yet it sets off a chain reaction of negative thoughts about the past.

Here is the good news. It is quite common for this to occur. It happens all the time. We never truly forget all of our experiences in life. They often come back from our memory to haunt us or give us trouble, and they usually come at the most inopportune time. What do you do with all those old memories . . . those ghosts from the past? You make friends with them. You acknowledge that they are there. You own them. They are yours. But at the same time you must make peace with them. You use them as stepping-stones of growth that remind you of things you shouldn't do in the future. They are experiences that you can share with others so that they can be spared similar hurt. Or they can be used to help others see how God delivered you from problems, and how He can deliver them. When you face the reality of the experiences, accept the truth of your hurt and anger, and make peace with what you cannot change, the memory remains but the pain goes away.

God grant me the serenity to accept the
things I cannot change, the courage to
change the things I can; and the wisdom
to know the difference.

Killing the Giant

Over 400 years ago, John Bunyan wrote *Pilgrim's Progress*. He wrote this classic allegory while in the dungeon of Bedford Prison in England for preaching the gospel. Prisons of those days did not have air-conditioning, color TV, and weight rooms. The food was not served on clean trays, and there were no electric lights. It was, to say the least, a very depressing place.

In his story, Christian Pilgrim is on his way to the Celestial City (heaven) to see the Good King (God) and to see the Good Prince (Jesus). On his way to the city, Pilgrim has many dangerous adventures. As the story goes, he became very lonely as he walked the Straight and Narrow Path. Finally, one day another pilgrim comes along. His name is Hopeful.

Pilgrim and Hopeful have a great time walking and talking together until they encounter rocks in the path. It became increasingly difficult to walk along. Soon they begin to talk less and less about the Good King and the Good Prince, and more and more about the rocks in the path.

One day Pilgrim sees another path that is going the same direction. It is blocked by a rock wall. The other path does not have any rocks or obstacles on it.

"Let's climb over the wall and walk on the broad, smooth path. There are no rocks there," said Pilgrim to

Hopeful. Hopeful thought that they should stay on the Straight and Narrow Path. After much discussion, they climbed the wall and started to walk the broad, smooth path. They were having such a good time that they did not see the sign next to the smooth path that said "By-path Meadow." Soon the broad path turned away from the Straight and Narrow Path.

It wasn't long before it became stormy. It began to rain. Pilgrim and Hopeful hid themselves under some old boards. In the morning they awoke to a terrible, loud noise. It was the sound of the footsteps of the Giant of Despair. He grabbed them both and cast them in the dungeon of Doubting Castle. They remained in the dungeon for many months. Often they would talk of how stupid they were to stray from the Straight and Narrow Path. They longed to escape from the grip of the Giant of Despair.

The giant had a wife by the name of No Faith. She hated pilgrims. She tried to convince her husband that he should go to the dungeon and kill the pilgrims. However, he was sort of a "Chicken Little" and could not bring himself to kill them. Instead he would taunt them. He would tell them that they would never get out of the dungeon of Doubting Castle. He told them that they should kill themselves. The giant would show Pilgrim and Hopeful the bones of all the other pilgrims who had died in the dungeon of Doubting Castle. He did this day after day, and they became very discouraged. Bunyan writes, "And many pilgrims die there."

One day Pilgrim remembers that he was given a key at the Palace Beautiful. He had been told that this key would unlock any door. He tells Hopeful how stupid he was to not use the key earlier. They both went to the dungeon door and tried the key. It worked. The door opened. They proceeded through the castle opening door after door. Finally, they came to the last door.

They turned the key and the latch made a loud clicking sound. The door squeaked as it opened. The sounds awoke the Giant of Despair, and he came running after them. He was not about to let go of them without a fight. Pilgrim and Hopeful ran for their lives. The giant was gaining on them.

Just as the Giant of Despair was about to grab them again, he saw the key in Pilgrim's hand. The sight of the key caused the giant's knees to buckle, and he fell to the ground in a cloud of dust. Pilgrim and Hopeful ran with everything they had in them. They climbed back over the wall and got back on the Straight and Narrow Path. They vowed never to let go of the key. Would you like to know what the key was called? The key was called "The Promises of God," the key that would unlock any door.

Have you been caught by the Giant of Despair? Have you been cast in the dungeon of Doubting Castle? Have you been taunted by the giant to kill yourself because there is no escape? You have been given a key to escape. It is called the Promises of God. Will you choose to use the key, or choose to remain in the dungeon?

> I am leaving you with a gift—peace of mind and heart! And the peace I give isn't fragile like the peace the world gives. So don't be troubled or afraid (John 14:27).

> Don't worry about anything; instead, pray about everything; tell God your needs and don't forget to thank him for his answers. If you do this you will experience God's peace, which is far more wonderful

than the human mind can understand. His peace will keep your thoughts and your hearts quiet and at rest as you trust in Christ Jesus (Philippians 4:6,7).

Dear God,

There are days that I would just like to escape from it all. I feel like pulling the covers over my head and having everything disappear. I feel like I am sinking in quicksand and there is no way out.

I guess I didn't realize how hurt I was. Not only am I hurt, but I am angry. Sometimes I just don't think it is fair the way things turn out. It shouldn't be that way. And yet it is that way.

God, I am having a hard time accepting the facts. I struggle with wanting revenge. I want repayment, but I know that no price can erase the pain. I think that the Giant of Resentment is almost as big as the Giant of Despair.

I am really tired of hurting. Please help me to make peace with my pain. Help me to bear the burden of unfairness. Help me to release my anger. Help me to forgive and not hold grudges. Help me to believe Your promises.

Depression Evaluator

❑ 1. I have been doing more crying lately, or I feel like crying.
❑ 2. I have been experiencing a lot of sadness lately ... sometimes for no reason I can put my finger on.
❑ 3. I have lost hope. I feel out of control of my life.
❑ 4. My motivation level has dropped dramatically.
❑ 5. My interest level has dropped, even in things that I usually enjoy doing.
❑ 6. I have been wondering if life is worth living. Even possible thoughts of suicide have crossed my mind.

❑ 7. I have noticed a change in my sleeping habits. I have a lot of restlessness at night, or I sleep too little, or I sleep too much.

❑ 8. Food has lost much of its taste. My appetite has decreased.

❑ 9. I don't seem to have much patience. I have been very irritable.

❑ 10. I have experienced anxiety, worry, and nervousness lately.

❑ 11. My usual energy level has dropped from what is normal.

❑ 12. I find it hard to get up in the morning. Morning is a difficult time.

❑ 13. I spend a lot of time thinking about my life and my relationships with other people. I play events over and over in my mind.

❑ 14. I think that I look and feel sad a great part of the time.

❑ 15. I have a poor self-image. I don't feel happy with myself.

❑ 16. I think a lot about the past. I have lots of hurts and regrets.

❑ 17. I have not been feeling very good. I have had headaches, an upset stomach, and back pains. Sometimes I have constipation, rapid heartbeat, and twitches. I have had a lot of neck pain.

❑ 18. My basic functioning in life is not up to par. I think that other people have even noticed a change in me.

_____ Total Boxes Checked

If you have checked nine or more boxes, it is recommended that you should talk with someone about the situations and hurts you are facing. It would be good to get another viewpoint. You may be holding in too much, and it is beginning to affect the way you think and function. The longer you put off dealing with what is concerning you, the worse it will get.

Don't put it off. Deal with it today. Today is the beginning of the rest of your life.[1]

Depression comes from hurt, loss, anger, or guilt that has been turned inward and has not been dealt with.
—R.E. Phillips

Discussion Questions

1. What role do you think self-pity plays in depression?
2. What causes hurt in the life of an individual? Why does hurt turn to anger? What place can the Bible have in dealing with hurt and anger?
3. How does someone develop a positive outlook on life rather than a negative one? Can a pessimist become an optimist?
4. What role do sinful thoughts and behaviors play in depression?
5. How can a spirit of thankfulness change depression?

Activities to Do

1. I have felt sad and depressed for

   _____
   (period of time)

2. I remember the following hurtful event that took place

   _____
   (location & time)

Describe what happened: _____

_____

_____

_____

_____

3.   ❏ I have not resolved the event or issue that
        took place.
     ❏ I have resolved it.

4.   I have the following signs of depression:
     Physical signs _____

     _____

     _____

     Emotional signs _____

     _____

     _____

     Spiritual signs _____

     _____

     _____

5.   I need to make peace with the following situa-
     tion(s) or forgive the following individual(s):

     _____

     _____

     _____

     _____

6.   I need to accept the following situation(s) and
     let go of replaying what cannot change. I need
     to move on with my life and make peace with
     pain: _____

     _____

     _____

     _____

     _____

7. Confess your sinful response to hurt or an unfair situation. Our reaction to an event is just as important as the event itself.

8. Begin to listen to good, wholesome Christian music. Music is a great help in making a joyful heart.

9. Stop watching so much TV. There are four causes of housewife depression in the United States: ABC, NBC, CBS, and Fox. The soap operas, talk shows, and various programs are often more depressing than uplifting.

10. Go help someone else. Nothing pulls you out of depression as much as doing kind deeds for others. It helps to eliminate self-pity. When you visit a dying or sick friend in the hospital, it will help to put your problems in perspective. Dr. Karl Menninger was asked at a meeting what a person should do if he felt a nervous break-down coming on. The famous psychiatrist said, "Lock up your house, go across the railroad tracks, and find someone in need and do something for him."

11. Put some laughter in your life. Laughter balances your emotions. Laughter keeps you from taking your life too seriously.

> Happy people choose to avoid waiting too long to see the funny side of their disappointments.
> —Andrew Matthews

12. Begin a program of reading the Bible. Mark all the promises you read. A promise is something to be believed. Remember, the promises of God are the key that will unlock the door to all problems.

Do you want more and more of God's kindness and peace? Then learn to know him better and better. For as you know him better, he will give you, through his great power, everything you need for living a truly good life: he even shares his own glory and his own goodness with us! And by that same mighty power he has given us all the other rich and wonderful blessings he promised (2 Peter 1:2-4).

Verses to Look Up

Psalm 27:13,14

Psalm 38:3,4,6,8

Isaiah 41:10

Matthew 11:28-30

John 14:27

Philippians 4:13

1 Thessalonians 5:18

2 Timothy 1:7

CHAPTER FIVE

The Battle with Anger

Whenever you are angry, be assured that it is not only a present evil, but that you have increased a habit.

—*Epictetus*

I will never forget Carla. She is one of the most colorful persons I have ever counseled. She was of average height, very strong, and extremely angry. I had been attempting to help her and her husband, who had been going through a very troubled marriage.

One day, in a fit of rage, Carla told her in-laws where they could go. She then told her husband where he could go also. It happened to be the same place. Carla slammed the door, stormed out of the in-laws' house, and walked home.

The in-laws told Jeff, her husband, that he shouldn't let Carla talk that way to them. He was the head of the house and should get her under control.

Jeff drove home and confronted Carla. They had a yelling match. I think Carla was winning because Jeff hauled off and hit her. She bounced off the dining room wall and fell to the floor. She scrambled to her feet, still yelling at Jeff, and ran into the kitchen.

Jeff ran after her. As he rounded the corner of the kitchen, he slipped on the linoleum and fell to the floor on his back. Carla quickly grabbed a butcher knife and jumped on his chest. She stuck the point of the knife in his neck and actually drew blood. She said, "You move, you . . . bleep . . . bleep . . . bleep, and I'll kill you."

You will have to take my word for it, but Carla was quite capable and willing to kill Jeff. It was actually one of few times in their marriage where there was very clear communication between them.

Carla and Jeff were displaying the most destructive emotion . . . anger. The various shades of anger run from mild frustration and irritation, to rage and murder. Every day the media shows us the results of anger. We hear about battered families. We see burned-out cities. We read about blown-apart nations.

As we look back at the story of Cain and Abel, we see one of the strongest emotions being displayed:

> But for Cain and for his offering He had no regard. So Cain became very angry and his countenance fell. Then the LORD said to Cain, "Why are you angry? And why has your countenance fallen?" (Genesis 4:5,6 NASB).

The Hebrew word for *anger* in this passage carries the following concepts:

- to glow warm or kindle
- to blaze up with jealousy
- to burn, fret, or grieve
- to be displeased

Cain was filled with jealousy, envy, and covetousness when Abel's offering was received by God and his was rejected. These feelings of competition and rivalry are common in families from early childhood and into adulthood. I believe that his feelings of envy began to glow warm. Cain kindled the fire with unkind thoughts. He fanned the embers of jealousy into a blazing fire of emotions. Cain's displeasure grieved him. He fretted over it until it burst into the inferno of murder.

Anger can destroy in a moment a relationship that has taken years to build.

Wise King Solomon said, "It is harder to win back the friendship of an offended brother than to capture a fortified city. His anger shuts you out like iron bars. Those who love to talk will suffer the consequences. Men have died for saying the wrong thing!" (Proverbs 18:19,21).

Dr. Henry Brandt, one of the nation's leading psychologists, suggests that anger is involved in 80-90 percent of all counseling. I would agree with him.

The consequences of anger have destroyed many relationships, many families, and many nations. How many families have gotten into heavy arguments in the process of going to church to worship God? How many hurt each other over issues such as washing the dishes, squeezing the toothpaste tube in the middle, or spilling a glass of milk? How many have had their self-image destroyed over school grades, athletic abilities, or their looks? The number is countless. Seldom does anger create healing.

The Faces of Anger

I had a friend in school who would bang his fist on the table and yell, "I'm not mad! I'm not mad! I'm not mad." Somehow we had a hard time believing him. Why do people have such difficulty dealing with anger? How can they see the anger in others and not in themselves? It is because the emotion of anger is viewed by most individuals as a negative response. Some even view their anger as being totally out of control. Others think that it is a mentally unhealthy feeling. A great many people think that if they admitted to being angry that it would be the same as saying, "I'm a bad person."

Rather than admitting that we are mad or angry, we say, "I'm a little out of sorts" or "I'm annoyed." We might even say that we are frustrated. With a little more pressure, we might admit that we are uptight, irritated, or exasperated . . . anything but angry or mad.

I remember as a small boy that I once told my brother I hated him. My mother overheard and said, "Robert, you can say that you dislike your brother, but never say that you hate him." Any display of strong emotions tends to threaten everyone who is nearby. We are not taught from childhood how to deal with angry emotions. The bottom line at that time was I hated my brother.

Every human being experiences the emotion of anger. Anger can manifest itself in either passive or active expressions. Passive anger usually takes place within the individual himself. Active displays are outward and often involve other people.

"You never come home on time. This is the third night this week that dinner is cold. I'm sick and tired of your inconsideration," said Betty to Jim. "Yeah, that's the thanks I get for busting my rear end trying to put food on the table for my family."

Basic Anger Responses:

1. We express anger.
2. We repress anger.
3. We confess anger.

Betty and Jim both felt that they were not appreciated. They were hurt and responded by expressing their anger. They were quite used to yelling at each other. Their caustic comments and sarcastic retorts had become a way of life. Sarcasm comes from the Greek word *sarkasmos*, which means "to tear flesh like dogs," or "to gnash the teeth in rage." Individuals who are more driving and expressive in their social styles have a tendency to let others know how they feel.

Sam, on the other hand, would never say anything when he was upset. He would become silent. He would sulk as he buried himself in the newspaper or as he escaped in a television program. His wife, Eileen, would respond in a similar manner. She would always find something to do in the kitchen or sewing room when she was mad. There was ominous silence and avoidance in their home when trouble was brewing. Both Sam and Eileen would repress their anger. They would stuff it deep inside.

I have found that it is a little easier to counsel two yellers rather than two silent people. At least with the yellers you know where they're at with their emotions. They are quite up front with their feelings. The quiet ones are more difficult. You are never quite certain what they are thinking. You have to expend significant energy fishing for feelings. Calm, still water runs deep.

You just don't know how deep. Those who are more analytical or amiable in their social behavior often repress their feelings.

Anger is an attempt at real contact. It is the fastest way to get others involved with you.

The third response to anger is to confess it. Those who confess their anger, first of all own it. They take responsibility for their emotions and try to speak the truth in as loving and honest a way as they can. Their driving motivation is to resolve the conflict rather than to punish the other person. They are not out for retaliation or revenge.

Those who confess their hurts and anger have a heart for forgiveness. They are looking for reconciliation and restoration. They have a willingness to grow and learn from trying situations. They do not operate in the attack mode or the denial mode.

Actions Speak Louder Than Words

Dick sat in the chair expressionless. His arms were folded over his chest and his legs were crossed. Charlotte, his wife, was discussing their marriage. It wasn't hard to tell that Dick was angry, even though he did not say a word.

Body language is often a giveaway of the true emotions that we are feeling inside. A long sigh, a roll of the eyes, a snort—they tell the true story of what we are thinking and experiencing. Gritted teeth, forced smiles, and looks of disgust are dead giveaways of the angry thoughts with which we are dealing.

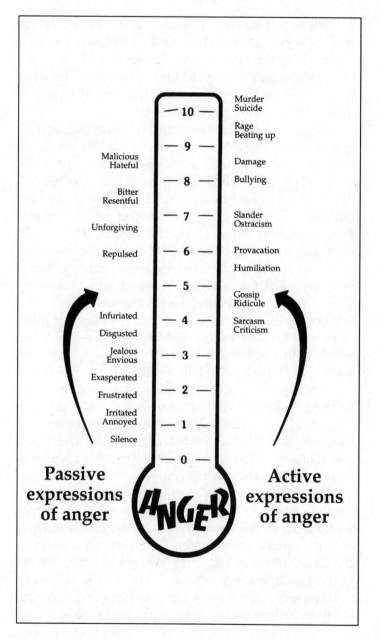

Angry actions convey angry thoughts even though words are not spoken. We have all witnessed the shaking fist with the raised center finger. This physical display is not meant to carry the idea of love and happiness. It is a message of anger and disgust. This is especially true when swearing accompanies it.

Anger can be displayed in boredom, negligence, and passive resistance. You can ask a person to do some task for you and he might agree to do it. He might even smile while talking with you, but his failure to show up on time or to complete the job may indicate his repressed anger at you or the project. Procrastination, chronic forgetfulness, and being accident-prone can also be nonverbal expressions of anger.

Some forms of humor carry anger and aggressiveness. When Bart was at the party and said, "When my wife sits around the house, she sits *around* the house," he was conveying more than one message. Was Bart really upset that his wife was putting on some weight? When Bart said to a fellow employee, "Is that your face or did your neck throw up?" it had a caustic sting. When Bart saw his friend and said, "I used to have a suit like that. Someday they will come back in style. I was just kidding, you know." Was he? The book of Proverbs says, "A man who is caught lying to his neighbor and says, 'I was just fooling,' is like a madman throwing around firebrands, arrows and death!" (Proverbs 26:18).

Flattery can be an expression of anger. It is a way a person can smile, say something nice, and still harbor resentment at the same time. "Flattery is a form of hatred and wounds cruelly" (Proverbs 26:28). Anger can take the form of "oozy sweetness" that creates guilt or obligations in others.

Anger can be expressed in behaviors that strike out at individuals or society in general. Graffiti on buildings is one way to express hostility. For the past year and a half we have had to paint our office building weekly to keep ahead of words, symbols, and gang names. Rudeness in traffic or in public meetings is a way to strike back at people. Alcohol and drugs can be a form of getting even. Often the drugs and alcohol lower inhibitions and reveal the true character of the person. There are more angry drunks than happy drunks.

Physical Effects of Anger

When anger is stuffed inside and not dealt with, it can have serious effects on the physical body. Hatred, bitterness, and resentment can produce or make worse many physical ailments. There have been studies that correlate anger and glaucoma. It has long been known that emotions of resentment have a direct effect on duodenal ulcers, peptic ulcers, nausea, and vomiting.

Low-back pain, constipation, and migraine headaches have a strong relationship to the pressures we face and our attitudes toward them. That is why we make statements such as, "You're a pain in the neck . . . or a little lower." "I get a headache just being around you." "I'm stuck in this situation and can do nothing about it."

Our emotions can have an effect on eczema, hives, cold and moist hands, runny nose, asthma, diarrhea, and high blood pressure. Dr. S. I. McMillen in his book *None of These Diseases* suggests that there are at least 57 diseases that can be made worse by our negative emotions. This does not mean that all illness is caused by anger. It does mean that sickness can be made more severe by holding hidden hatreds, grudges, and an unforgiving spirit. When there are hostilities, sickness can be a way to withdraw or escape from an undesirable situation. Sickness can be used to make others feel sorry or guilty

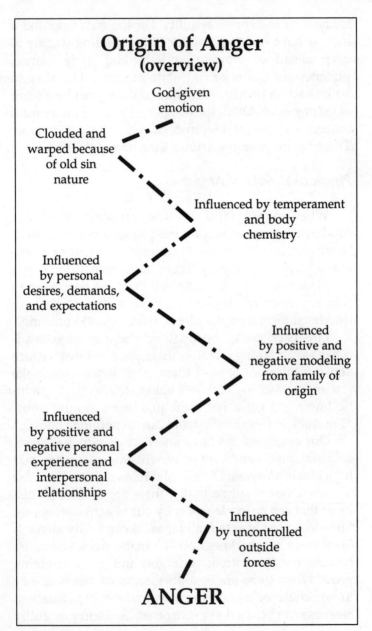

Origin of Anger
(overview)

God-given
emotion

Clouded and
warped because
of old sin
nature

Influenced by temperament
and body
chemistry

Influenced
by personal
desires, demands,
and expectations

Influenced
by positive and
negative modeling
from family of
origin

Influenced
by positive and
negative personal
experience and
interpersonal
relationships

Influenced
by uncontrolled
outside
forces

ANGER

for the way they have treated us. Sickness can also help us to avoid some task or responsibility. We can also use sickness as a way to get back at someone.

It has long been understood that our eating patterns have much to do with our emotions. Some people have an intense fear of becoming obese and starve themselves (anorexia nervosa). Others go on eating binges, followed by self-induced vomiting (bulimia). Many people simply stuff food into their bodies the same way they stuff down angry thoughts and feelings.

A relaxed attitude lengthens a man's life;
jealousy rots it away.
—Proverbs 14:30

Over the years, I have had people tell me about various relatives or acquaintances they knew who were very godly. They would say things like, "I never saw them get mad." "They were never angry." "They were the nicest people I ever met." I would then ask them about these people's health. Did they have much sickness in their lives? Often the reply would be affirmative. My educated guess is that sometimes we misread as godliness the repressing of emotions that manifests itself in sickness.

I'm reminded of the story of the pastor who played golf with one of his elders. When the elder hit the golf ball in the sand trap, he swore. When the pastor did the same thing he was silent. When the elder hit the ball into the water hole, he got mad and broke his club. When the pastor did the same thing, he was silent and calm. When the elder missed a putt, he threw a temper tantrum. When the pastor missed the putt, he simply

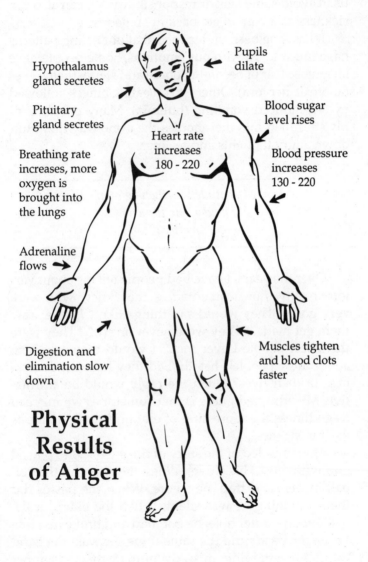

Hypothalamus
gland secretes

Pupils
dilate

Pituitary
gland secretes

Blood sugar
level rises

Heart rate
increases
180 - 220

Breathing rate
increases, more
oxygen is
brought into
the lungs

Blood pressure
increases
130 - 220

Adrenaline
flows

Digestion and
elimination slow
down

Muscles tighten
and blood clots
faster

Physical
Results
of Anger

smiled. Finally, the elder said, "Pastor, I really admire you. When things go wrong on the golf course you just remain silent, calm, and smile." "That's true," said the pastor, "but where I spit, the grass dies."

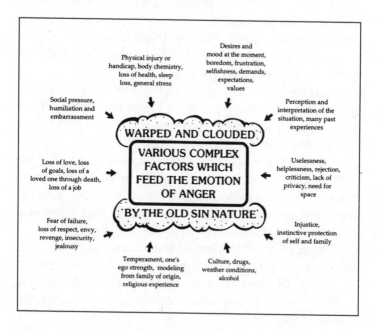

The Focus of Anger

The emotion of anger is an equal-opportunity provider. It can get angry at anything or anyone. We can become angry with God, parents, or authority figures. We don't like to have anyone else tell us what to do or control our lives.

We can turn our anger toward our mate, our children, or our friends. We can become angry with strangers, especially while driving our car. We can even get angry with ourselves. We call ourselves names and tell ourselves how stupid we are. We can focus anger on real or perceived danger or various obstacles in our path. We can even get angry at inanimate objects. Men get angry an average of six times a week and women three times a week. Studies show that men get angrier at inanimate objects and women get angrier at people. Women think it is silly to throw a screwdriver or kick a wall. Men think it's a waste of time to get upset over people.

You've heard the story about the man who was yelled at by his boss. He went home and yelled at his wife. She, in turn, yelled at her child. The child then kicked the dog, and the dog chased the cat.

Most anger is misplaced or misdirected. People love to blame others since it gives them an excuse to start or continue unacceptable behavior. It lets them off the hook for their actions. God forbid that I become responsible for my own words and behavior!

Often only 25 percent of the anger has to do with the current situation. Past hurts and disappointments make up 75 percent of the expressed anger. Instead of emptying a wastebasket of feelings, we dump the whole garbage truck.

When expectations become unreasonable and dreams are not fulfilled, anger is born.

Much of our anger arises because of unspoken expectations. We are disappointed that plans and relationships don't go as we would like them to. We get upset at having to wait in long lines or being slowed by heavy traffic when we are in a hurry. We have unrealistic expectations about life. It would be like me saying, "I should never have to wait in a line. How dare there be anyone ahead of me!" Or I might say while I am driving, "Get out of the way. Here comes King Me. No one should block my path." I might even go on to comment, "Everyone must like me. No one should disagree with me."

"That's ridiculous," you say. I agree. We place ridiculous demands on ourselves and other people. The more we live in a fantasyland, the more disappointed we will become. Part of our anger at being a victim of unfairness is because we have created an unreal world in our minds. We are responsible for setting ourselves up to be victims, to be hurt.

Why Do I Get Angry?

When you find a lump in your body, you immediately become concerned. Could it be cancer? You set up an appointment with your doctor and go in for some tests. He takes a sample of the growth and sends it in for a biopsy. And then you wait.

When the day arrives, you are nervous as to what the answer will be. Your doctor asks you, "Would you like me to not tell you the results, or would you like me to make up something?" "No," you respond, "I want to know the results. Even if it is bad news, I want to know the truth. Don't lie to me."

I am going to tell you the painful truth about anger. I will pull no punches. I hope that you will bear with me. It won't be pleasant. It will take some adjustment to get used to it.

The root cause of anger is selfishness. We want what we want, when we want it. We want others to respond as we want them to. We want the circumstances in our lives to all work according to our plans.

We want to always be happy. We want God to change life so that it proceeds the way we think it should. When none of the above happens, we become angry.

I was angry with my friend:
I told my wrath, my wrath did end.
I was angry with my foe:
I told it not, my wrath did grow.
—William Blake

King Ahab in the Bible gives us a classic example of anger and selfishness. He saw something he wanted and got angry because he couldn't have it.

Naboth, a man from Jezreel, had a vineyard on the outskirts of the city near King Ahab's palace. One day the king talked to him about selling this land.

"I want it for a garden," the king explained, "because it's so convenient to the palace." He offered cash or, if Naboth preferred, a piece of better land in trade.

But Naboth replied, "Not on your life! That land has been in my family for generations."

So Ahab went back to the palace angry and sullen. He refused to eat and went to bed with his face to the wall!

"What in the world is the matter?" his wife, Jezebel, asked him. "Why aren't you eating? What has made you so upset and angry?"

"I asked Naboth to sell me his vineyard, or to trade it, and he refused!" Ahab told her.

"Are you the king of Israel or not?" Jezebel demanded. "Get up and eat and don't worry about it. I'll get you Naboth's vineyard!" (1 Kings 21:1-7).

Ahab's anger and selfishness led to the murder of Naboth and the taking of his land.

In the thousands of hours of counseling that I have experienced, I have never had anyone come into my office and say: "You've got to help me. My spouse is too good to me. They are too loving. They are too gentle. They are too kind. I can't stand their acts of goodness anymore. I want a divorce." You see, two unselfish people never get a divorce.

"Just a minute," you say. "Isn't anger a natural response?"

"Yes. It is a natural response, but it is not always a godly response."

"Isn't there such a thing as righteous indignation and proper anger at injustice in life?"

Of course there is. But if we are both honest, that happens very seldom in our experience. Rarely are we angry in the same way God is, and still more rarely do we respond in the loving way that Jesus would. Most of our anger is because we don't get our way. We don't think people should treat us as they do.

On a number of occasions I have asked various audiences to raise their hands if they have been hurt by others. Everyone raises their hands. I then ask for a show of hands of those who deliberately hurt others. Almost no one raises their hands. Something is wrong. Everyone is hurt but no one is doing the hurting. It helps to point out how inward we have become.

The Bible has much to share about anger. It gives God's viewpoint on this powerful emotion. The Bible gives us instruction for dealing with anger:

> Stop your anger! Turn off your wrath. Don't fret and worry—it only leads to harm (Psalm 37:8).

> But when you follow your own wrong inclinations your lives will produce these evil results: impure thoughts, eagerness for lustful pleasure, idolatry, spiritism (that is, encouraging the activity of demons), hatred and fighting, jealousy and anger, constant effort to get the best for yourself, complaints and criticisms, the feeling that everyone else is wrong except those in your own little group—and there will be wrong doctrine, envy, murder, drunkenness, wild parties, and all that sort of thing. Let me tell you again as I have before, that anyone living that sort of life will not inherit the Kingdom of God (Galatians 5:19-21).

> Dear brothers, don't ever forget that it is best to listen much, speak little, and not become angry; for anger doesn't make us good, as God demands that we must be (James 1:19,20).

You need to openly and honestly face your hurts and angers. You need to acknowledge that anger is a sin. It does not promote goodness and the well-being of others. It is deadly and destructive. If anger would produce happiness, the whole world would be delirious.

You need to confess your anger to God. If you are going to get victory over your temper, you will need God's help. Ask Him to help remove the angry habit pattern that has developed over the years. Repeat this process each time you see the ugly head of anger rising out of the pool of selfishness. Always keep in mind that anger is only one letter from danger.[1]

> Stop being mean, bad-tempered and angry. Quarreling, harsh words, and dislike of others should have no place in your lives. Instead, be kind to each other, tenderhearted, forgiving one another, just as God has forgiven you because you belong to Christ (Ephesians 4:31,32).

> If you are angry, don't sin by nursing your grudge. Don't let the sun go down with you still angry—get over it quickly; for when you are angry you give a mighty foothold to the devil (Ephesians 4:26,27).

Dear God,

I'm really blown away when I think about my temper. It is so easy for me to give way to my angry feelings. I can't believe how powerful a force it is. Sometimes I attack people and destroy them with my sharp tongue—even the ones I love.

God, I have been holding bitterness and resentment for so long that I don't know how to let go of it. I have been swimming in the whirlpool of hurts that people have caused me. I have tried to stay afloat by grabbing the straws of unfairness and injustice. They don't hold me up. I'm sinking with my grudges.

Help me to stop being mean and bad-tempered. Help me to forgive those who have hurt me. Help me to learn to become kind and gentle in what I say and do. I can't do it without Your help. I've tried too many times on my own. Help me to let go of my desires for revenge.

Today I give up. I need You to rescue me.

Anger Inventory

*At the heart of every problem you will find
the easiest answer to its solution.*

Listed below are 25 potentially upsetting situations. Use the simple rating scale and estimate the degree of irritability you would normally feel if the event happened to you. Place the number on the line after each illustration. Upon completion, total your score and see how you measure up on the Anger Inventory.

0 It does not bother me—I feel little annoyance.

1 It bothers me a little—I feel irritated.

2 It moderately bothers me—I feel upset.

3 It makes me quite angry—I feel my stomach tighten.

4 It makes me very angry—I see red.

1. You have someone cut in front of you while you are waiting in line. _____

2. The car in front of you is moving very slowly and you cannot pass. _____

3. You are playing a volleyball game and one of your teammates misses the ball and you lose the game. _____

4. Your friend or spouse is talking to you and saying phrases like, "You always," "You never," or "Every time you." _____

5. You are in the doctor's waiting room, it is an hour past your appointment time, and you are still waiting. _____

6. You are in a hurry to get somewhere and your car has a flat tire, making you very late. _____

7. You can't get away from a pushy, aggressive salesman from whom you don't want to buy anything. _____

8. You have just found out a friend has shared an unkind rumor about you. _____

9. Someone interrupts you and won't let you finish what you were talking about. _____

10. You're at a party and someone publicly embarrasses you and everyone laughs. _____

11. You have a lot of work to do at the office, but keep getting interrupted, and you can't meet your deadline. _____

12. Your mate or friend forgets to mail an important package for you and it costs you money. _____

13. You come out of the store and find that someone has put a dent in your new car. _____

14. You brush against a door that has been freshly painted and ruin a new leather coat. _____

15. You are studying for an important test and your roommate has the radio playing loud rock music. _____

16. Your friend has lost a special item of clothing or broken something you loaned him. _____

17. You get up off a park bench and rip your pants. _____

18. You are trying to clear up an important matter, when the person you are talking to on the phone hangs up on you. _____

19. You drive downtown to pick up an appliance you ordered. When you get there, you realize you left your checkbook at home. _____

20. You are standing on a corner waiting for the light to change when a truck splashes mud on your new clothes. _____

21. Your spouse or friend asks you to meet him at a certain time and fails to show up. _____

22. Someone keeps staring at you and won't look away. _____

23. You get blamed for something that happened at work, and it was not your fault. _____

24. You step on some dog droppings just before you have to go to an important interview. _____

25. A bum on the street calls you a name when you won't give him some of your change. _____

0-45   You have outstanding control of your responses.

46-55   You are above average in handling pressure.

56-75   You are average in control of your emotions.

76-85   You get quite irritable with most annoyances.

86-100   You win the prize as the Grand Master of anger. Your reward is tension headaches, high blood pressure, and the loss of respect from family and friends. Only a few people get into as much trouble and as out of control as you do. You are a true Irritability Champion.[2]

A man's wisdom gives him patience;
it is to his glory to overlook an offense.
Proverbs 19:11 NIV

Discussion Questions

1. Is all anger sinful? What is the place for legitimate anger?

2. How does one deal with all the angry thoughts and feelings that come to mind, and not sin or violate the principles of Scripture?

3. Are there times we should express our anger rather than repressing it? Are there times when we should repress our anger rather than expressing it? How is it done?

4. What do the following words mean to you: *discussion, argument, quarrel, fight*? What is the difference between hostility, malice, bitterness, resentment, hatred, and wrath?

5. What positive steps have you taken with your anger? How have you dealt with other people's anger in a positive way?

Activities to Do

1. This next week keep a written record of the times that you experience the emotion of anger. Note when (time of day) the anger occurs. Note the focus of your anger (family, friends, yourself, God, inanimate objects, etc.). Look for a pattern as you lose your temper. Do you need to

talk with someone? Do you need to ask forgiveness? Do you need to forgive someone? Do you need to let go of some situation, grudge, or resentment?

2. My most difficult anger experience this last week was _____

_____

_____

_____

_____

3. I did or said the following wrong things: ____

_____

_____

_____

_____

4. If I had it to do over I would respond by ____

_____

_____

_____

_____

5. I think that God allowed this situation to come into my life to teach me _____

_____

_____

_____

_____

6. The fruit of the Spirit includes the virtues of love, joy, peace, patience, kindness, goodness, faithfulness, gentleness, and self-control. I

would like to work on the following fruit this next week: _____. I will try to do the following steps: _____

_____

_____

_____

_____

7. I want to see the following things changed in my life with regard to my anger and temper:

_____

_____

_____

_____

Verses to Look Up

Proverbs 14:17,29

Proverbs 15:1,18

Proverbs 17:14

Proverbs 19:11,19

Proverbs 22:24

Matthew 5:23,24

Matthew 18:15-22

Romans 12:19,20

Colossians 3:8

1 Peter 3:8-17

CHAPTER SIX

Understanding Your Feelings

Never apologize for showing feelings. Remember that when you do, you apologize for the truth.

—*Benjamin Disraeli*

Not long ago, I was speaking to a geologist. His job consists of trying to discover underground water. He searches the cracks and fissures of the earth looking for crystal-clear water.

I asked him what was the best well he had found. He said that he had found several, one of which provided over 1200 gallons per minute. He went on to say that his favorite one was an artesian well that produced 750 gallons per minute.

An artesian well requires no pump. The water in the artesian well is already under pressure. This pressure forces the water up to the surface without mechanical help. It comes from an underground river that flows on its own, seeking to be released.

Deep within the soul of man is an artesian wellspring of emotions. These emotions flow like a great underground river. They seek the surface, looking for release.

Cain could be called "the father of mental illness" because we see in his life the roots of the behaviors and emotions that lead to what is commonly called "dysfunction." Cain was faced with an uncomfortable situation. He could have chosen to respond favorably, but instead chose the negative response. Cain felt his strong emotions as they sought release:

> But for Cain and for his offering He had no regard. So Cain became very angry and his countenance fell. Then the LORD said to Cain, "Why are you angry? And why has your countenance fallen? If you do well, will not your countenance be lifted up? And if you do not do well, sin is crouching at the door; and its desire is for you, but you must master it" (Genesis 4:5-7 NASB).

As these artesian emotions reach the surface and are released, they produce emotional waterfalls that pour into a lake of feelings. The emotional waterfalls seem to have three primary sources: the flow of anger, the flow of peace, and the flow of fear.

As these strong emotions strike the lake of feelings, they sometimes blend together, making it difficult to tell the source. The strong currents in the lake of feelings depend on which emotional waterfall is flowing the hardest.

When we look at a waterfall in real life, it captures our attention. The water sometimes strikes rocks on its way down and forms ever-changing cascades. Depending on the time of day we look at a waterfall, we may see rainbows in the mist. Even as we focus on where the water strikes a particular rock on the cliff, we notice changes. The water never quite splashes the

same way. In similar fashion, our emotions have subtle variations and never react quite the same way.

Rocks on the Cliff of Life

Although the emotional waterfalls may flow from one primary source, we will not always notice subtle variations. Upon a closer look, we see the flow of emotions strike the rocks of daily circumstances, family of origin, and our own personality, our social style, interpersonal relationships, and uncontrolled outside forces. As the primary emotion strikes the problem rocks on the cliff of life, splashing variations occur. These variations represent different shades of meaning from the primary flow.

Primary flow:	*anger*
Shades of meaning:	ill-tempered, huffy, furious, cranky, cross, spiteful, infuriated, unforgiving, silent, irked, annoyed, disgusted, sarcastic, miffed, sore, uptight, burned-up, exasperated, grumpy, out of sorts, mad, resentful, envious, loathing, frustrated, irritated, jealous, mean, critical, uptight, annoyed, bitter, hateful, malicious
Primary flow:	*peace*
Shades of meaning:	joyful, pleased, poised, zestful, praise-filled, humorous,

hopeful, excited, productive, confident, active, secure, curious, possessing a clear conscience, upbeat, fun-loving, positive, independent, self-assured, patient, courageous, happy, optimistic, having a good attitude

Primary flow: *fear*

Shades of meaning: overwhelmed, sad, upset, dread-filled, anguished, possessing low self-esteem, dependent, fatigued, miserable, uneasy, frantic, troubled, morbid, untrusting, timid, discouraged, negative, strained, withdrawn, jumpy, silent, nervous, weighed down, apprehensive, doubt-filled, panic-stricken, phobic, tense, anxious, stressed, worried, fretful, afraid

Why Do I Feel the Way I Do?

The purpose of this book is to help you understand your emotions and to cope with life. It is important that we understand that all of our emotions are God-given. They can be our best friends or our worst enemies.

You may say, "I can understand how peace, joy, and happiness are good friends. But I don't see how anger and fear are my friends at all."

Anger and fear are our friends because they tell us what is important in life. They alert us to the fact that something may be wrong. They are strong motivators that can save or destroy us. Anger and fear are raw energy.

Let's say you were crossing the street. Suddenly, you look up and see a large truck. It is moving toward you rapidly. The energy emotion you first will feel is fear. Fear will be your enemy if you freeze on the spot. Fear will be your best friend if you jump out of the way of the truck.

Anger can be your worst enemy, especially if you tell your boss off or hit a family member. Anger can be your best friend if it helps you use your anger energy to protect your wife who is being mugged. Anger will be a friend if you get angry enough at yourself to change a bad habit.

Are you ready to face your feelings? Are you ready to experience the richness of your emotions? Are you ready to grow and change in your outlook toward life?

How Do I Get Overwhelmed by My Emotions?

"I've been depressed for weeks. I don't feel like doing anything. Sometimes I just sit and stare into space. I don't think life is worth living. I think it would be better if I were gone. My family has a good life insurance policy on me, and they would be better off if I were not here. I don't feel like trying anymore." It was easy for me to see that Carl was at the end of his rope as he sat in my office. Carl had been hurt financially when a joint partnership that he was in went bankrupt.

"I've never really been able to please my mother. I could never do anything right." Sharon had been coming for several counseling sessions and was suffering from a low self-image. "I don't have very many friends in school. I guess you could call me a loner. I've always been alone."

Our feelings can bring us joy or cause us much pain. It is the painful side of our emotions that have prompted this book. Is there a way to not be overcome by painful emotions? Is there something I can do before the psychiatrist comes, before the men in little white coats come and carry me off to the funny farm?

To help keep yourself out of the funny farm (mental hospital), it is important to understand how your emotions work. Especially difficult to understand is the negative side of the powerful emotions of anger and fear.

I believe that the whole process of emotions begins with the core of some type of *great love or affection* or the ownership of some possession. This core is usually real, but it could also be assumed to be real. Either way, the same emotions will be felt by you.

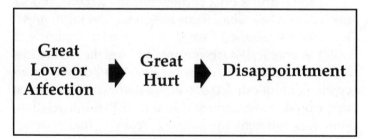

Circling around the core are personal assumptions, perceptions, expectations, attitudes, needs, and demands. These attitudes and perceptions may be conscious or unconscious to you. You may express them, or they may be held in and unexpressed.

When love or affection has been violated, or when

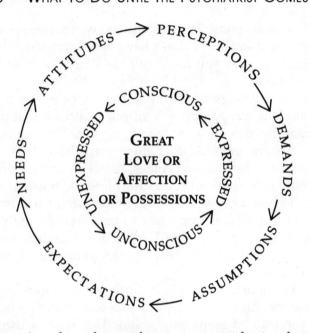

possessions have been taken away, *great hurt or loss* is felt.

If some drunk on a corner calls me a name, it does not hurt me. "So what! Same to you buddy! Who cares!" But when someone I love or have a relationship with calls me a name, it hurts me greatly. I feel the hurt or loss and am *disappointed*. This is because I had different perceptions about our relationship. I had expectations that this would never happen. I assumed that our relationship was different than that. I believed that I would always have my possession.

My emotions of *anger or fear* then arise. I become angry with that person for what they said or did. Or I may become fearful that there is loss and our relationship is destroyed. I feel like fighting, or I feel like fleeing. I may feel it was extremely unfair that my possession has been taken away. When these emotions are not properly dealt with, I feel *frustration*. I become defensive and protective because I am hurt.

These defensive or protective reactions may cause me to *attack* the individual directly. "I don't like the way you talk to me. You have no right to embarrass me that way in front of others." Or I may hold my anger and hurt inside. I think about it. I dwell on it. It eats me up. I may choose revenge, procrastination, forgetfulness, sabotage, or silence. I may choose resentment, bitterness, or hatred.

I may, on the other hand, not want to face the situation or the individual who has hurt me. I will *withdraw* physically, mentally, or emotionally. "I can't face them. I can't go through any more hurt. The pain is too great." I may retreat into silence and a world of loneliness. I may suffer a slow death inside my mind.

When attack or withdrawal does not solve the problem, I may try forms of compromise. I may try to *compensate* by drawing attention to a favorable behavior or characteristic. This will divert attention away from my unfavorable behaviors or characteristics. I don't want people to see my faults, so I will magnify my good points. This will help me not to face issues that need to be changed in my life.

I may *rationalize.* I will try to justify my behavior by giving seemingly plausible reasons for my negative conduct—death before dishonor. God forbid that I should be responsible for my actions!

I may choose *substitution.* Since I am having trouble with a particular relationship, I will substitute it with another relationship or situation that I can deal with or have success in. That way I won't have to face the issue that is really causing me difficulty.

I may choose *projection.* If I can call attention to other people's failings, it will lessen attention to my failings. If I do it loud enough and long enough, I may not have to deal with the fact that I am part of the problem.

I can also choose to *daydream* and have a fantasy about how my problems should turn out. Or I can become the suffering martyr and thereby become the hero or heroine of the story. I might even *repress* all of the hurt and pain and pretend like it is not there. I can bury my head in the sand and pretend that none of the hurt exists and the pain is not real.

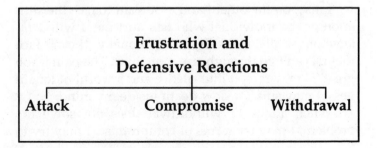

**Frustration and
Defensive Reactions**

Attack   Compromise   Withdrawal

Attack, withdrawal, and compromise do not resolve the hurt and pain. They seem to increase and prolong it. The increase of hurt and the lengthening of time one is in pain seem to lead to *depression* and *anxiety*. Depression is filled with *anger*, hurt, loss, and guilt. Anxiety is filled with *fear*, hurt, loss, and guilt.

When you are hurt long enough by people or the loss has been great, you develop a *lack of trust* in people. As trust ebbs away, *loss of respect* grows. As loss of respect grows, *resentment* increases. As resentment increases, *hatred* and *bitterness* are born.

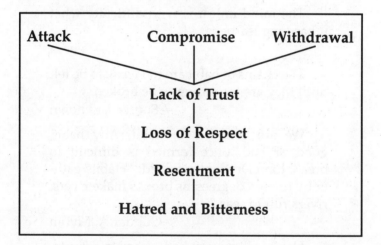

If the process of great hurt and loss . . . anger and fear . . . frustration and defensiveness . . . depression and anxiety . . . and loss of trust and bitterness is repeated over and over enough times, the individual develops a *habit pattern of response*. This habit pattern develops into a lifestyle of dealing with conflict.

In the next chapter we will explore examples of those who have chosen to establish lifestyle patterns. See if you can identify anyone you know.

It seems, in fact, as though the second half of a man's life is made up of nothing but the habits he has accumulated during the first half.

—Fyodor Dostoevsky

Habit, if not resisted, soon becomes a necessity.

—Augustine

Habits are at first cobwebs, then cables.

—Spanish proverb

The mind unlearns with difficulty what it has long learned.

—Seneca

The chains of habit are too weak to be felt until they are too strong to be broken.

—Source Unknown

We are creatures of habit. Any habit, good or bad, once formed is difficult to break. John Dryden once said, "Habits gather by unseen degrees, as brooks make rivers, rivers run to seas."

—Gundar A. Myran

Habit is like a soft bed—easy to get into, hard to get out of.

—Kelly Fordyce

Habit is a shirt of iron.

—Source Unknown

Habit is habit, and not to be flung out of the window by any man, but coaxed downstairs a step at a time.

—Mark Twain

It is easy to assume a habit; but when you try to cast it off, it will take skin and all.
—Henry W. Shaw

The person who has been born into God's family does not make a practice of sinning, because now God's life is in him; so he can't keep on sinning, for this new life has been born into him and controls him—he has been born again.

—1 John 3:9

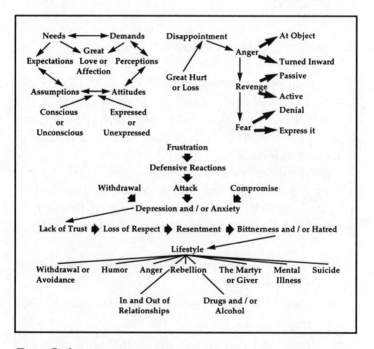

Dear God,

I think I am beginning to realize that I have some habits that need to be changed. It seems like such a big task. I am not quite sure that I am up to it. My spirit is willing but my flesh is weak.

Please give me the strength and determination to conquer habits that have come into my life. Help me to learn a new way of responding to the problems that I face on a daily basis.

I know that if I am going to have success, it will come through Your help. Please help me to establish positive habits for spiritual, emotional, and physical health.

Please help me to be honest with my feelings. Help me not to run from them. Help me to not be overcome by my feelings.

God, do You make house calls?

Hurt Evaluation Quiz

Sometime this week, participate in a Hurt Evaluation Quiz. Set aside about a half an hour and find a quiet place alone. Take your Bible, a pad of paper, and a pen with you. At the top of the paper list a particular hurt that you have experienced.

Next ask yourself the following questions. As you ask each question, write your answer down on the pad of paper. By writing your answers down, it will help you to sort out and have an objective look at your hurt.

1. How did you respond to the particular hurt? What did you do?

2. List two other ways that you could have responded.

3. How did you contribute to this situation? Did you say or do something to bring the problem on or make it worse? Be honest. Very few people are totally innocent victims. It does happen, but it is rare.

4. Are you holding any jealousy, hatred, or bitterness in your heart? Are you angry with someone in particular? If so, write the name or names down.

5. List four possible ways that the hurt could be dealt with now.

6. Which of the four ways would be the best one for you and everyone involved? Write down why you think this way would be best.

7. Which way do you think God would like you to choose? Which way are you going to choose?

8. Do you need to ask someone for forgiveness for your negative attitude? Do you need to forgive someone? Who are these people? Write their names down.

9. Take a moment and pray for those you need to forgive. Ask God to forgive you for the hostile feelings you have been holding deep within you. Write their names down and pray for these people this next week.

10. Write down your plan of attack for resolving the hurt, letting go of the hurt, or accepting the hurt.

Verses to Look Up

Psalm 119:9-11	Galatians 2:20
Jeremiah 17:9,10	Philippians 2:13,15
Luke 10:9	2 Timothy 2:15
Romans 6:11-14	James 4:7,8

CHAPTER SEVEN

Lifestyles of the Not-So-Rich-and-Famous

Having problems may not be so bad. We have a special place for folks who have none—it's called a cemetery.

—*Frank A. Clark*

Rita has always been shy. As a small child she was teased a lot at school. She would cry and run away and hide. She always hated any kind of conflict. When her parents would argue, she would go to her room. Rita has a difficult time expressing her opinions. She would rather be hurt herself than confront anyone about an issue. Rita has developed a well-organized routine for dealing with various hurts, disappointments, and pain. Rita *withdraws* or *avoids* them. She pretends that they do not exist.

Cary is almost a walking, talking, stand-up comedian. He is always up on the latest joke or story. He was the class clown in school. He is the inventor of wild practical jokes. He is the life of the party. In fact, there is very little in life that Cary takes seriously.

Cary never seems down. Sometimes Cary's friends wonder if he is for real. How could any person be that happy? Cary learned early in life to cover his hurts with *humor*. Cary may tell a lot of puns, but deep inside he is really punishing himself.

Fred is someone you want to avoid. He is a very angry man. He is an equal-opportunity provider. He will get equally angry with anyone he meets and who crosses him. Fred will get mad at drivers in front of him on the freeway, salesclerks, and his wife and children. Fellow employees avoid Fred because they don't like being chopped to pieces. The people at Fred's church and social clubs don't appreciate his put-downs. Fred was hurt as a child. Fred was hurt as a teenager. He has not been happy about it. He has always struck back at those who have hurt him with *anger*. Watch out—Fred is an explosion about to happen.

Anger is never sudden. It is born of a long, prior irritation that has ulcerated the spirit and built up an accumulation of force that results in an explosion. It follows that a fine outburst of rage is by no means a sign of a frank, direct nature.
—Cesare Pavese

Sara has always been a little different. She does not like the word *no*. She struggled in school and ran with the wrong crowd. She always spoke her mind and talked back. Just when her *rebellion* started no one is quite sure. Sara did not get along well at home, at school, or with anyone in authority. She got into trouble with the police and ran away from home. It is hard for people to see how deeply Sara is hurt. They only see her lashing out. Sara is different than Fred, who reacts at those who cross him. Sara strikes out at anyone and everyone, even innocent people.

Linda's lifestyle is certainly not one of anger. Linda will do anything for you. She goes out of her way to be helpful. But she will not let you help her. If you helped her, you might no longer be obligated to her. Linda has experienced a lot of pain and suffering. Her life seems like one big hurt. One might suspect that she enjoys hurt. Some of her friends think that she might even create hurtful situations. Some people call it attention-getting. Others call it self-pity. In any case, Linda thrives on it, encourages it, and seems to enjoy the lifestyle of the *martyr* or *giver*.

Bruce chose the popular lifestyle of going crazy. Bruce did not choose *mental illness* right away. He started with fears and phobias. He graduated to irresistible impulses such as washing his hands ten times a day and counting the number of times he said *and*. He then went on to repeat certain words over and over. To that he added paranoia. He believed the police had wiretapped his house and that everyone was out to get him. His arms became paralyzed, he lost his memory, and now he sits very still. His eyes are lifeless, and he has escaped from the pain and hurt of life into the land of the living dead.

Mental illness is a myth whose function is to disguise and thus render more palatable the bitter pill of moral conflicts in human relations. In asserting that there is no such thing as mental illness, I do not deny that people have problems coping with life and each other.
—*Thomas Szasz*

John is a very handsome man. He has dated lots of girls. But his relationships do not seem to last. It is true that he was hurt in one relationship, but that was long ago. It seems that just as a new relationship moves to a point of commitment, something happens. The relationship blows apart. It is almost like John sabotages the relationship. Then he steps back and responds, "You're just like the others." Doesn't it seem strange that all the girls are the same? Could it be that maybe John is the one who is the same? John moves in and out of jobs the same way he moves *in and out of relationships.* John has not been able to face his hurt and conquer his fears.

Jack doesn't attack people with his anger. He is not humorous like Cary. He is not rebellious like Sara, nor does he move in and out of relationships like John. Jack has chosen a different way to deal with his hurt. Jack handles his disappointments with *alcohol and drugs.* When Jack is "high" he feels no pain. He is brave and can conquer the world. Jack has not escaped from the burden of hurt and pain. He has only exchanged it for bondage to a monster that destroys him from within.

Debbie was hurt deeply over a broken love affair. But it did not stop there. Her boyfriend started dating her best friend. Then she was hurt twice and became angry. However, she never expressed her anger. She just held it in, thought about it, and nursed it. And her anger grew. Soon Debbie was overcome with hurt, grief, and anger. It was all she thought about. The hurt she felt drained all of her energy. She was depressed. She saw no escape from her pain. Debbie no longer cries. There are no more tears left. Debbie is sitting alone in her car with the motor running. Debbie has chosen to end her lifestyle with *suicide.*

As you look at the emotional chart, can you identify your lifestyle? Part of beginning to counsel yourself is to identify where you are. Can you think of situations

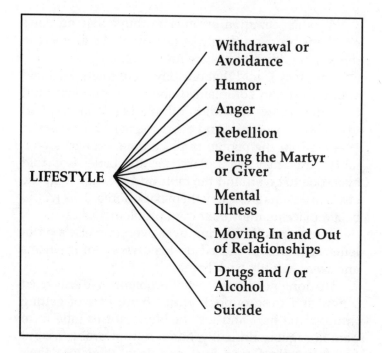

where you were hurt or where there was a big loss in your life? Can you see how you responded to that hurt or loss?

The Golden Key to Problems

I must confess that I don't know anyone who is not hurting. Pain is "in" this year. Why am I telling you this? It is because I want you to see that you are not alone. Everyone has struggles and problems. I mean *everyone.* Join the club. Welcome to the human race.

It is a common error to think, "I shouldn't have problems. I shouldn't feel this way. Something is wrong with me. I must be crazy." In reality, you are crazy when you say, "I have no problems."

Another common error is to think that no one's problems are as difficult as our own. We all tend to think that our problems are the worst.

The story is told that one day all of mankind stood before God and complained about the problems and trials they faced. They didn't think that what they had to deal with was fair. And everyone asked for relief.

God told the people to place their problems on a table. After they were placed on the table, God told everyone to go around the table and pick up someone else's problems and carry them back home. This would be a replacement for their own problems.

After carefully looking over everyone else's problems, each person picked up his own set of problems and went happily back home.

We don't need a new set of problems. We only need a new and fresh outlook at our own. Part of getting through the hurt and loss of life is not to hide from pain nor ignore difficulty, nor run from problems, but face them. In facing hurt and loss, they lose their power over us. We need to learn to accept the hurts and make peace with them.

Is that information disappointing? Were you expecting a golden key to unlock the pain door? Were you looking for a rose garden? Are you looking for the easy way out of being part of the human race?

Here then is the golden key: *There is no easy way!* Part of what makes life so interesting are the difficulties that make us grow . . . even when we don't want to.

What would it be like if we went to play golf and the course was just one big long grass rectangle as far as you could see? There would be no sand traps. No water holes. No trees. No doglegs or turns. No hills and valleys. The game would not be as interesting.

As we move forward in this book, I hope you will

come to appreciate your problems. The difficulties on the golf course of life are not to destroy us, but to make us more skilled and polished. They make life full and rich. They help us to grow and mature. And they give us opportunities to share with others what God has taught us.

Has any man ever obtained inner harmony by simply reading about the experiences of others? Not since the world began has it ever happened. Each man must go through the fire himself.
—*Norman Douglas*

The following was printed in the *Manchester Guardian* with the caption, "So You Think You Have Problems?"

When I got to the building I found that the hurricane had knocked some bricks off the top. So I rigged up a beam with a pulley at the top of the building and hoisted up a couple of barrels full of bricks. When I had fixed the building, there were a lot of bricks left over. Then I went to the bottom and cast off the line. Unfortunately, the barrel of bricks was heavier than I was, and before I knew what was happening the barrel started down, jerking me off the ground.

I decided to hang on and halfway up I met the barrel coming down and received a hard blow on the shoulder.

I then continued to the top, banging my head against the beam and getting my fingers jammed in the pulley. When the barrel hit the ground, it burst its bottom, allowing all the bricks to spill out.

I was now heavier than the barrel and so started down again at high speed. Halfway down, I met the barrel coming up and received severe injuries to my shins.

When I hit the ground, I landed on the bricks, getting several painful cuts. At this point I must have lost my presence of mind because I let go of the line. The barrel came down, giving me another heavy blow on the head and putting me in the hospital.

I respectfully request sick leave.

Turn Up the Thermostat

Every man and woman who walks the face of planet earth encounters problems and trials of varying degrees. No one can or will escape problems. What you do with your problems is what counts. You can be like either the thermometer or the thermostat. The thermometer is influenced by outside hot or cold forces. The thermostat, on the other hand, controls the heat or cold. You *can* be a thermostat person when it comes to outside problems. Jesus, in His high priestly prayer in John chapter 17, did not ask the Father to remove us from this world of problems. He asked the Father to keep us safe in the middle of the problems.

Did you know that God is not caught unaware by your difficulties? Did you know that Jesus is "panic proof?" There is not a situation in life that Jesus cannot handle if you commit it to Him. "For I know whom I have believed, and am persuaded that he is able to keep that which I have committed unto him against that day" (2 Timothy 1:12 KJV).

There is not a problem that enters your life from a broken fingernail, to a run in your nylons, to a flat tire, to a test at school, to broken eyeglasses, to pain in your body——there is nothing that happens to you as a member of His family, that isn't first checked out by the heavenly Father. There is no happenstance in your life, only circumstances.

Do you ever feel like you have been picked on? Do you ever look up to heaven and say, "Why me?" If you do, you are normal. But please don't fall for Satan's line of argument. He will say that you have a special problem that no one else has.

> But remember this——the wrong desires that come into your life aren't anything new and different. Many others have faced exactly the same problems before you. And no temptation is irresistible. You can trust God to keep the temptation from becoming so strong that you can't stand up against it, for he has promised this and will do what he says. He will show you how to escape temptation's power so that you can bear up patiently against it (1 Corinthians 10:13).

"If God has the power to make a way of escape, why doesn't He just remove the problems altogether?" Because the truth is, that the only way you can develop in your Christian life is through trouble.

> Dear brothers, is your life full of difficulties and temptations? Then be happy, for when the way is rough, your patience has a chance to grow. So let it grow, and don't try to squirm out of your problems. For when your patience is finally in full bloom, then you will be ready for anything, strong in character, full and complete (James 1:2-4).

If I were to ask you if you wanted a stronger faith, you would probably say, "I certainly would." Wonderful! Then plan on some extra problems because the only way your faith gets strengthened is through problems—from a breakup with your boyfriend to a divorce situation. Remember that every one of the problems in your life has first been filtered by the Father.

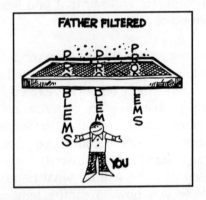

God's Presence in Our Problems

Have you ever felt like quitting? Have you ever had the desire to escape from the problems of life? Well, join the club. If there is any comfort in numbers, everyone has felt this way at some time in his life. Maybe you feel this way now.

The psalmist David expressed his desire to escape from problems when he said,

> My heart is in anguish within me. Stark fear overpowers me. Trembling and horror overwhelm me. Oh, for wings like a dove, to fly away and rest! I would fly to the far-off deserts and stay there. I would flee to some refuge from all this storm (Psalm 55:4-8).

The problems of life are like earthquakes that quickly arise and seem to overpower us. It is in the midst of these earthquake-problems that God wants to come to our aid with instruction and encouragement.

> In my distress I screamed to the Lord for his help. And he heard me from heaven; my cry reached his ears. Then the earth rocked and reeled, and mountains shook and trembled. How they quaked! For he was angry. Fierce flames leaped from his mouth, setting fire to the earth; smoke blew from his nostrils. He bent the heavens down and came to my defense; thick darkness was beneath his feet. Mounted on a mighty angel, he sped swiftly to my aid with wings of wind. He enshrouded himself with darkness, veiling his approach with dense clouds dark as murky waters. Suddenly the brilliance of his presence broke through the clouds with lightning and a mighty storm of hail (Psalm 18:6-12).

David had an earthquake-problem. David cried for help. David received help. But did you notice that God veiled His approach? It was at the point when clouds (problems) were the darkest that the glory of the Lord shone through.

Are the clouds dark for you, friend? Have you cried to God for help? Do your earthquake-problems look like "murky waters"? Then praise God! The brilliance of God's presence is not far away.

The Refiner's Fire

He sat by a fire of seven-fold heat,
As He watched by the precious ore,
And closer He bent with a searching gaze
As He heated it more and more.

He knew He had ore that could stand the test,
And He wanted the finest gold
To mold as a crown for the King to wear,
Set with gems with a price untold.

So He laid our gold in the burning fire,
Though we fain would have said to Him, "Nay,"
And He watched the dross that we had not seen,
And it melted and passed away.

And the gold grew brighter and yet more bright;
But our eyes were so dim with tears,
We saw but the fire—not the Master's hand—
And questioned with anxious fears.

Yet our gold shone out with a richer glow,
As it mirrored a Form above
That bent o'er the fire, though unseen by us,
With a look of ineffable love.

Can we think that it pleased His loving heart
To cause us a moment's pain?
Ah, no! but He saw through the present cross
The bliss of eternal gain.

So He waited there with a watchful eye,
With a love that is strong and sure,
And His gold did not suffer a bit more heat
Than was needed to make it pure.

— *Author Unknown*

So be truly glad! There is wonderful joy ahead, even though the going is rough for a while down here. These trials are only to test your faith, to see whether or not it is strong and pure. It is being tested as fire tests gold and purifies it—and your faith is far more precious to God than mere gold; so if your faith remains strong after being tried in the test tube of fiery trials, it will bring you much praise and glory and honor on the day of his return. You love him even though you have never seen him; though not seeing him, you trust him; and even now you are happy with the inexpressible joy that comes from heaven itself. And your further reward for trusting him will be the salvation of your souls (1 Peter 1:6-9).

Dear God,

There are some days that I would be content to play the golf game of life on a level field. I think that I would even like a few days with no sand traps, water holes, or twists and turns.

I know that I become a more skilled player with problems. I know that they help me to mature and grow. I think that I am just tired. I need a second wind or some extra energy.

Please blow a little energy my way. I want to change my lifestyle. I want to play by Your rules. Help me to get into Your guide book, the Bible.

Teach me how to live a happy life right in the middle of problems.

Emotional Awareness Exercise

Place a check in the boxes beside the emotional reactions you have experienced in the last month.

Emotional Reactions of Anger

- ❑ Ill-tempered
- ❑ Cross
- ❑ Irked
- ❑ Sore
- ❑ Exasperated
- ❑ Resentful
- ❑ Frustrated
- ❑ Annoyed
- ❑ Bitter
- ❑ Spiteful
- ❑ Disgusted
- ❑ Huffy
- ❑ Furious
- ❑ Grumpy
- ❑ Uptight
- ❑ Mad
- ❑ Envious
- ❑ Jealous
- ❑ Hateful
- ❑ Mean
- ❑ Cranky

Total Checked _____

Emotional Reactions of Peace

- ❑ Joyful
- ❑ Zesty
- ❑ Hopeful
- ❑ Secure
- ❑ Possessing a clear conscience
- ❑ Positive
- ❑ Happy
- ❑ Pleased
- ❑ Praise-filled
- ❑ Excited
- ❑ Curious
- ❑ Upbeat
- ❑ Self-assured
- ❑ Cheerful
- ❑ Poised
- ❑ Humorous
- ❑ Confident
- ❑ Creative
- ❑ Fun-loving
- ❑ Patient
- ❑ At ease

Total Checked _____

Emotional Reactions of Fear

- ❑ Sad
- ❑ Possessing a low self-image
- ❑ Uneasy
- ❑ Untrusting
- ❑ Discouraged
- ❑ Jumpy
- ❑ Doubt-filled
- ❑ Worried
- ❑ Anguished

❑ Withdrawn
❑ Apprehensive
❑ Anxious
❑ Dread-filled
❑ Dependent
❑ Troubled

❑ Fatigued
❑ Morbid
❑ Timid
❑ Nervous
❑ Panic-stricken
❑ Fretful

Total Checked _____

Is there an emotional pattern to your reactions? Have you checked more boxes in the area of anger, peace, or fear? Maybe this is an area that you need to be alerted to and work upon.

My lifestyle response to problems and difficulties seems to be:

❑ Humor
❑ Drugs/Alcohol
❑ Withdrawal or avoidance
❑ Anger
❑ Suicidal thoughts

❑ In and out of relationships
❑ Rebellion
❑ Mental illness
❑ Being the martyr or giver

Discussion Section

1. How realistic is it to think that life should be problem-free?

2. If you could trade away your own problems, whose problems would you like to have? Your employer's? Your relatives'? Those of the mayor of your city? Those of the president of the United States? Other?

3. What is the role of optimism or pessimism in the problems you face?

4. How did your family members deal with their problems? How did they react under pressure?

5. In what ways do you respond to problems in ways similar to your family? Are you happy with your actions? What behaviors would you like to change?

Activities to Do

I would like to change the following in my emotional reactions: _____

_____

_____

_____

_____

I have gained the following insight about my emotions:

_____

_____

_____

_____

_____

Notes:_____

_____

_____

_____

_____

Verses to Look Up

Matthew 11:28

John 14:1

John 16:33

Romans 8:28

Romans 8:37-39

2 Corinthians 1:3

Hebrews 4:15

1 Peter 2:21-24

1 Peter 5:7

Revelation 3:10

CHAPTER EIGHT

Taking Responsibility

> *Responsibility is the thing people dread most of all. Yet it is the only thing in the world that develops us, gives us manhood or womanhood fiber.*

—*Frank Crane*

"I've told you a million times not to leave your bike lying in the middle of the driveway," yelled Dennis to his son Danny. "You'll learn your lesson this time. You're not allowed to ride your bike for a month!"

"I think that is a little harsh," said Lisa, Dennis's wife.

"It's time he grew up and took some responsibility around here. I don't want to hear any more about it!"

Dennis didn't want to address the fact that he was dumping an extra amount of anger on his son. He had lost a business deal that he had been working on for the last three weeks. Just before Dennis went home, his boss called him into his office and "raked him over the coals" for losing the account. When Dennis saw the bike in the driveway, it was the last straw. He blew up and let Danny have it. He justified his harsh actions by telling Lisa that Danny needed to learn to accept responsibility.

Jan had been trying to lose weight for several months. It had been a real battle for her. On Tuesday she went shopping at her local supermarket. When she passed the cookie aisle she said to herself, *Just because I'm on a diet, doesn't mean the rest of the family is. I'll buy them some cookies and ice cream for dessert.* That afternoon when she was putting the groceries away, she noticed the cookies. *I've done such a good job on my diet for the last week. I haven't eaten any snacks. I think I will treat myself. It's my reward for being so faithful.* Jan enjoyed her cookies and soothed herself with rationalizing that she deserved a reward. Who could argue with that logic?

"What a jerk," said Carl as he slammed the door and threw his books on the table. "What's wrong?" asked his mother. "I failed Dr. Carlson's biology test." "Didn't you study for it?" "Of course I did. I was up till two o'clock last night." "Oh, that's too bad. That's a long time to study for a test. Maybe there is some way you can make it up." "Not with that idiot Dr. Carlson. He wouldn't help anyone." Carl was feeling down. He was angry. Yet he was also not completely honest. When he said that he was up till two o'clock last night, his mother should have asked, "When did you start studying?" Carl would have had to answer, "One thirty." You see, Carl had been watching TV early in the evening. He then was on the phone in his room talking to his friends until 1:00 A.M. Next he took a shower and got ready for bed. When he crawled into bed at 1:30 A.M., he opened his book and studied until he got sleepy at 2:00 A.M.

Justification, rationalizing, covering, and lying have become a way of life. It is easy to drop into the world of half-truths. We learn early in life how to make excuses and shift the blame—anything but accept responsibility for our actions. Cain didn't want to accept responsibility for his attitude and behavior, either:

> But for Cain and for his offering He had no regard. So Cain became very angry and his countenance fell. Then the Lord said to Cain, "Why are you angry? And why has your countenance fallen? If you do well, will not your countenance be lifted up? And if you do not do well, sin is crouching at the door; and its desire is for you, but you must master it." And Cain told Abel his brother. And it came about when they were in the field, that Cain rose up against Abel his brother and killed him. Then the LORD said to Cain, "Where is Abel your brother?" And he said, "I do not know. Am I my brother's keeper?" (Genesis 4:5-9 NASB).

The Hebrew word in verse 7 for "do well" carries the concepts of being happy, being successful, doing the right thing, and cheerfulness. This is an amazing concept. God is saying that if you want to be happy, live a godly life. Do the right thing. He goes on to say that if we don't do the right thing, "sin is crouching at the door." In plain English, "When you don't do what you are supposed to be doing, there is going to be trouble and problems awaiting you."

Ninety percent of our problems would disappear if we would be doing what we should.

How many family arguments would disappear if everyone was doing what he or she should at home?

How much tension would go away if simple things were done by family members?

Hanging up clothes	Cleaning up rooms
Taking out the trash	Helping with the dishes
Cleaning the garage	Sharing toys
Doing homework	Showing consideration
Respecting each	for others
other's privacy	Saying kind things

Wouldn't it be interesting to see if we could "out-love" our family and friends? You see, life is not as complicated as some people suggest that it is. It may be difficult, but it is not complicated. Doing our duty would eliminate a host of difficulties. King Solomon stated the same concept when he said,

> Young man, it's wonderful to be young! Enjoy every minute of it! Do all you want to; take in everything, but realize that you must account to God for everything you do. . . . Here is my final conclusion: fear God and obey his commandments, for this is the entire duty of man. For God will judge us for everything we do, including every hidden thing, good or bad (Ecclesiastes 11:9; 12:13,14).

An excuse is worse and more terrible than a lie;
for an excuse is a lie guarded.
—Alexander Pope

Excuses are used to cover or hide the true reason behind behavior. It is accomplished by either avoiding the truth or not telling the whole truth. When someone uses an excuse, that person is hoping that it will help to free or exempt him from some obligation or duty. "I'm sorry that I am late. I got stuck in traffic" might be the excuse. What may be hidden is the fact that the person got a late start or really didn't want to be there in the first place. He may have known that if he would have been on time, that he would have had to help set up the room. He might not have wanted to meet a particular person, or a host of other unspoken reasons.

Excuses are an attempt to keep from facing reality. It may be a device to help protect oneself from uncomfortable or unpleasant circumstances. Excuses can help to cover failures and weaknesses. "I just don't understand computers. I leave that for young people. You know, you can't teach an old dog new tricks." The truth might be that someone is just lazy or doesn't want to take the time to read a book. He may be embarrassed to ask for help or let others see how little he knows.

An excuse often comes to mind when an individual feels some form of anxiety. It might arise because of an accusation or criticism. People may have observed his behavior and called attention to it. They may be "stepping on his toes" and touching a sensitive area in his life.

Often an excuse is worded so that the negative behavior has permission to continue: "She yelled at me first. If she didn't yell, then I wouldn't yell."

Sometimes excuses mask true motivation. The excuse is designed to confuse the hearer. It is a form of deception. A good excuse can be used to change the subject and divert the pressure. It can be used to help the listener forget the original question or observation: "How come you didn't show up for the meeting? I was really counting on you." "I would have been there but

George called. Did you know that George had to file bankruptcy? His wife, Claire, had to have an operation on her gall bladder also. She is having a rough time of it. Have you called them yet?" In a few clever maneuvers the original question is lost. The pressure is off. The question was not answered. Now the person can relax.

People who pride themselves for thinking logically sometimes even believe their own excuses. This is because they present the excuse in a rational, step-by-step way. They will get angry with anyone who challenges their excuse. They see any questioning of their excuse as a questioning of their logic. They do not accept that the excuse is being challenged; they only think they are being attacked on their deductive reasoning ability. Sometimes they're just plain hostile. Outbursts of temper help to keep anyone from questioning further. They have learned that anger usually helps them to get their own way.

When anxiety over a confrontation arises, excuses help the individual save face. The fear of embarrassment or the threat of punishment give rise to many excuses. A good excuse helps to alleviate guilt. Sometimes the guilty party will spend a great deal of energy trying to convince others that his actions and attitudes are justified.

Running from the Real Problem

Have you ever been woken out of a sound sleep by the ring of a telephone? You sometimes don't know where you are for a few seconds. When this happened to me, the voice on the other end of the phone said, "Bob, I'm sorry to wake you up, but we need your help. One of the guys in the high school camp has gone crazy. Could you come and help us?"

I quickly dressed and went to the dorm area. I could see someone with a flashlight waiting for me. "He tore up the dorm and then ran outside somewhere. I don't know where he is."

I told him to turn off his light and stop talking. Sound carries well at night, and soon we could hear voices coming from main camp. I said, "Let's go to where the sounds are coming from."

Upon arriving I could see about 18 to 20 people milling around. "Which one is he?" I asked. It was close to 1:00 A.M. in the morning.

It didn't take long before I knew. One of our night accommodations vans drove down the street on its way to work. As it passed a young man standing in the street, he reached out and hit the side of the van with his fists. "I think I know who he is," I said.

As I got closer to the young man, I could see in the dark that the other men had surrounded him in sort of a human corral. I walked up to him and introduced myself. I said, "I am Bob Phillips. Do you know who I am?"

"You're a doctor."

"No."

"You're a counselor."

"No. I'm the bottom line. I'm the camp director. The buck stops with me."

At that, he screamed and yelled that the demons were all over him. He started moving away from me and screaming some more. I tried to talk with him, but he was yelling and crying and would not listen.

I worked myself into a position directly in front of him and tried to communicate. He continued to yell about the demons and cried. I suddenly lunged forward, placing my arms around his shoulders, and pulling him into me. I held him in a viselike grip. I was not about to let go.

I am almost 6'2" and weigh about 190 pounds. This young man was taller and heavier than I am. I held him tight to get his attention and to keep him from hurting me. His right cheek was next to my right cheek. He was screaming about the demons in my right ear, struggling to get away, and crying at the same time.

It was during this intense process that I noticed it. His head was touching my head when all of a sudden he wiped the snot from his runny nose. In that split second I knew he was fully aware of everything that was happening to him. He didn't like the snot running down his face. He was in touch with reality.

I quickly yelled that I wanted everyone to leave and go to bed. Two other counselors and myself went to our administration building with the young man. Upon arriving, I held him for a while, like you would hold your son who had hurt himself. It wasn't long before he quieted down. We talked about the situation and what had triggered it. He had a number of reasons and excuses.

The bottom line was that he had acted like an idiot with the guys in his cabin and couldn't back down from the situation he had created. He had to continue to act crazy in order to save face. If he didn't respond with bizarre behavior, he would have had to admit that he was just acting. He would have been exposed. He would have had to take responsibility for his negative actions.

You see, people's pride will cause them to go to great extremes rather than admit that they are wrong. Once they make a scene, they have to protect their self-image. They will invent demons, scream and yell, and continue weird behavior as a mask for their true motivation. Excuses of stress and outside circumstances will be created to make other people believe that they are not responsible or in control.

What Goes Around Comes Around

The Bible gives many illustrations of the principle of "cause and effect." In Galatians 6:7-10 (NASB) we read,

> Do not be deceived, God is not mocked; for whatever a man sows, this he will also reap. For the one who sows to his own flesh shall from the flesh reap corruption, but the one who sows to the Spirit shall from the Spirit reap eternal life. And let us not lose heart in doing good, for in due time we shall reap if we do not grow weary. So then, while we have opportunity, let us do good to all men, and especially to those who are of the household of the faith.

One of the classic examples of disobedience, excuses, and cause and effect is the story of Saul in 1 Samuel 15:12-26. He had been anointed king, and the Lord instructed him to destroy Amalek and all that he had. Amalek is seen as a type of the flesh in the Old Testament. Saul was to destroy all that was fleshly (worldly).

Saul chose to ignore God's instructions. He rebelled by keeping the best of the animals alive. He also kept Agag, the king of the Amalekites, alive. He just wanted to do his own thing. When Samuel the prophet arrived on the scene, he found King Saul in the process of patting himself on the back for the victory:

> And Samuel rose early in the morning to
> meet Saul; and it was told Samuel, saying,
> "Saul came to Carmel, and behold, he set up a
> monument for himself" (1 Samuel 15:12 NASB).

Saul proceeds to compound his disobedience by lying and telling Samuel that he carried out the command of the Lord. Samuel confronts Saul and his behavior:

> But Samuel said, "What then is this bleat-
> ing of the sheep in my ears, and the lowing of
> the oxen which I hear?" (1 Samuel 15:14 NASB).

Saul starts speaking half-truths. He covers his failure. He attempts to divert Samuel's attention to confuse him with other issues.

> Then Saul said to Samuel, "I did obey the
> voice of the LORD, and went on the mission
> on which the LORD sent me, and have
> brought back Agag the king of Amalek, and
> have utterly destroyed the Amalekites."
> (1 Samuel 15:20 NASB).

Saul begins to excuse his behavior. He attempts to shift the blame to other people. If we can successfully shift the blame, it takes the pressure off us. Saul tries to escape responsibility for what he knew he should be doing. He endeavors to suggest that someone else is responsible for his temptation. James tells us where temptation comes from:

> And remember, when someone wants to
> do wrong it is never God who is tempting

him, for God never wants to do wrong and never tempts anyone else to do it. Temptation is the pull of man's own evil thoughts and wishes. The evil thoughts lead to evil actions and afterwards to the death penalty from God. So don't be misled, dear brothers (James 1:13-15).

But the people took some of the spoil, sheep and oxen, the choicest of the things devoted to destruction, to sacrifice to the LORD your God at Gilgal (1 Samuel 15:21 NASB).

Samuel quickly moves to the bottom line and speaks firmly and directly. He lets Saul know what God thinks. He helps Saul face the cause-and-effect relationship to his behavior:

And Samuel said, "Has the LORD as much delight in burnt offerings and sacrifices as in obeying the voice of the LORD? Behold, to obey is better than sacrifice, and to heed than the fat of rams. For rebellion is as the sin of witchcraft and insubordination is as iniquity and idolatry. Because you have rejected the word of the LORD, He has also rejected you from being king" (1 Samuel 15:22, 23 NASB).

When Saul hears his judgment for wrongdoing, he immediately attempts to become spiritual. I cannot count the number of times that when we caught young people doing things wrong, they started talking "church talk." When they knew they were facing ownership for their actions, they would attempt to convince you that they were serious and wanted to change. Why is it that positive changes in behavior are discussed after a person is caught rather than before he or she is caught?

> Then Saul said to Samuel, "I have sinned; I have indeed transgressed the commandment of the LORD and your words, because I feared the people and listened to their voice. Now therefore, please pardon my sin and return with me, that I may worship the LORD" (1 Samuel 15:24, 25 NASB).

Samuel is not convinced by all of Saul's spiritual talk. Saul still did not take ownership of his behavior. He still referred to the influence of the people on his decision. He was the king. He should have been influencing the people's actions. Samuel knew that Saul's cries for mercy were not from repentance and restitution. They were just "smoke and mirrors." He was saying the right thing, but he didn't believe the right thing. He was a great politician. Samuel makes Saul own his behavior. He makes him take responsibility for his actions:

> But Samuel said to Saul, "I will not return with you; for you have rejected the word of the LORD, and the LORD has rejected you from being king over Israel" (1 Samuel 15:26 NASB).

Let wickedness escape as it may at the bar,
it never fails of doing justice upon itself;
for every guilty person is his own hangman.
—Seneca

There are not many books written that address themselves to integrity, morality, and responsibility. There is a strong movement suggesting that morality is a relative thing. What may be moral to you may not be moral to me. There are no absolutes in life. This type of thinking leads to anarchy. Every man will do what is right in his own eyes.

Can you imagine what would happen if we attempted to play baseball, basketball, or football without any rules? If we didn't have any laws, how would society survive? What would traffic be like in a busy city without stoplights? It would be disaster. What would happen if I ignored the physical laws of nature that God has established? I would jump off a building and all the way down I would try and convince myself that I wasn't falling and that there wouldn't be a quick and deadly stop at the end of my fall.

Just as there are physical laws in nature, there are spiritual and moral laws. God established these laws in the heart of every man and woman entering this world. When the spiritual and moral laws are violated, individuals come face-to-face with the still, small voice of conscience:

> He will punish sin wherever it is found. He will punish the heathen when they sin, even though they never had God's written laws, for down in their hearts they know right from wrong. God's laws are written within them; their own conscience accuses them, or sometimes excuses them. And God will punish the Jews for sinning because they have his written laws but don't obey them. They know what is right but don't do it (Romans 2:12-15).

God spoke to Cain and told him that "sin was crouching at the door; and its desire is for you, but you must master it." You begin to master sin in your life by becoming obedient to the still voice of conscience. Cain refused to listen to the voice of God, and as a result he was separated from God and became a wanderer.

> I am more afraid of my own heart than of the Pope and all his Cardinals. I have a Pope within me, the great Pope, self.
>
> —Martin Luther

> I have lived my life with a perfectly good conscience before God up to this day.
>
> —Paul the apostle—Acts 23:1 NASB

> Holding to the mystery of the faith with a clear conscience.
>
> Paul the apostle—1 Timothy 3:9 NASB

> Keep a good conscience so . . . those who revile your good behavior in Christ may be put to shame.
>
> —Peter the apostle—1 Peter 3:16 NASB

> Having our hearts sprinkled clean from an evil conscience.
>
> —Hebrews 10:22 NASB

> I also do my best to maintain always a blameless conscience both before God and before men.
>
> —Paul the apostle—Acts 24:16 NASB

> Conscience . . . "the great beacon light God sets in all."
>
> —Robert Browning

A good conscience is a continual Christmas.
—Ben Franklin

Keep conscience clear, then never fear.
—Ben Franklin

There is no pillow so soft as a clear conscience.
—Source Unknown

There are many psychologists who talk about false guilt. They suggest that our parents warped us with dishonest messages. They give illustrations of mothers who say, "You never call me. Don't you love me anymore?" I am sure that there is such a thing as false guilt. But I really don't think that it is as big a problem as psychiatrists would like us to believe. What I am talking about is good, old-fashioned, true, and honest guilt. I am convinced that the reason why most people run around with a guilt complex is because they are guilty. The reason they are angry and their countenance is downcast is because they are not doing what they should.

They know deep inside that they have not been very loving to their family. They know they have said unkind things. They know they should be more patient. They know they have been putting off jobs that they should be doing. They know they have been stealing small items from work. They know they have been exceeding the speed limit. They know that they are making personal phone calls on company time. They know that they have been exaggerating, telling lies, and spreading gossip about other people. They know that they have not really been studying for their tests. They know they have not been completely honest with their income-tax forms and haven't listed all of their income, especially cash income. They know they should help a tired mate but don't do it. They know that they have flirted with the opposite sex, and it would not please their mates. They know they have yelled too much at the children and punished them unfairly.

The American Heritage Dictionary says that guilt is the "remorseful awareness of having done something wrong." The way we can tell that we have done something wrong is that our conscience will let us know. We just don't like to listen to that still, small voice. We hate to admit that we are wrong. If we admitted that we were wrong, we would have to assume responsibility for our actions.

Has your countenance fallen? Have you been angry? Have you had feelings of depression? Would you like to be bright with joy? Then may I suggest that you start doing what you should.

You say, "But Bob, how do I know what I should be doing?"

Ask God. He will tell you. He will take away all doubts of which direction you should take, or what you should be doing. The next time you find yourself in a questionable situation, ask the following questions:

- What would Jesus do in this situation?
- What would Jesus say to this person?
- How would Jesus respond to this need?

Sin is like a hungry lion. It is just waiting for you to get off the straight and narrow path. This lion wants to bring trouble and devastation to your life. You must conquer it. Remember, "Obedience is better than sacrifice."

Help me to do your will, for you are my God. Lead me in good paths, for your Spirit is good (Psalm 143:10).

You know these things—now do them! That is the path of blessing (John 13:17).

Dear brothers, don't ever forget that it is best to listen much, speak little, and not become angry; for anger doesn't make us good, as God demands that we must be. So get rid of all that is wrong in your life, both inside and outside, and humbly be glad for the wonderful message we have received, for it is able to save our souls as it takes hold of our hearts. And remember, it is a message to obey, not just to listen to. So don't fool yourselves. For if a person just listens and doesn't obey, he is like a man looking at his face in a mirror; as soon as he walks away, he can't see himself anymore or remember what he looks like. But if anyone keeps looking steadily into God's law for free men, he will not only remember it but he will do what it says, and God will greatly bless him in everything he does (James 1:19-25).

Dear God,

I find that it is really easy to make excuses for my behavior. I have become a professional at it. I have become the "blame master."

Help me to take responsibility for my actions. Please help me to become alert to the needs of those around me. Selfishness is so natural to me. Help me learn to be patient and forgiving.

My face has been downcast for a long time. Sin has not only been at the door, I think it has even come inside for dinner. I know that if there are going to be changes in my life, You are going to have to give me help.

I don't want to sit on the bench, disqualified for Your service. I want to be used by You. I want to help other people have their countenances lifted up also. Give me the strength to fight the lion of sin that seeks to devour me.

Responsibility List

1. Make a list of behaviors that you would like to see changed in your life: _____

_____

_____

_____

_____

_____

_____

_____

2. Make a list of behaviors that you would like to begin in your life: _____

_____

_____

_____

_____

_____

_____

_____

_____

3. Go back over the two lists you have just made. Decide which items you would like to begin with first. Put a 1, 2, 3, 4, etc. ranking order to the lists. Determine in your mind to begin today with the number 1 item mentioned on each list.

4. Make a list of the most common excuses you use. This will help you to become alert and responsible for your actions:

_____

_____

_____

_____

_____

_____

_____

_____

_____

_____

5. Spend a few minutes in prayer each day. Ask God to help you put away negative behaviors in your life and put on positive attitudes and actions.

Verses to Look Up

Genesis 22:1,2,9-13
Exodus 19:3,5; 24:7
Ezekiel 33:1-4,6,7
Matthew 5:20,41; 21:28-31

Luke 17:7-10; 22:39-42
Romans 5:19; 13:7-9
Hebrews 5:7-9

CHAPTER NINE

Understanding Yourself and Others

One learns people through the heart, not eyes or the intellect.

—*Mark Twain*

"You make me so mad I could spit!" said Mary to her husband, Ralph. "You can't make up your mind about anything. Why do I have to make all the decisions in this house? Why am I the one who always disciplines the kids? You just clam up and draw into a shell like a turtle. You run when there is any kind of conflict." Ralph looked at Mary and shrugged his shoulders. He continued to read the newspaper. She turned in disgust, slammed the door, and went to the bedroom in tears.

"Why don't you lighten up a bit and have some fun? Life doesn't have to run according to a set schedule," said Don to his wife, Lois. "In fact, I told the boys at work that I got up and went to the bathroom during the night, and when I came back that you had made the bed." Lois did not crack a smile. Her lips only pressed tighter together.

It would be easy to go on with one illustration after another of how people encounter stress with each other. The most difficult thing to deal with in life is a relationship that is not running smoothly. It is easier to have your house burn down or lose all your belongings in a flood than to go through struggles with people. Some people will even resort to physical violence.

> But for Cain and for his offering He had no regard. So Cain became very angry and his countenance fell. Then the LORD said to Cain, "Why are you angry? And why has your countenance fallen? If you do well, will not your countenance be lifted up? And if you do not do well, sin is crouching at the door; and its desire is for you, but you must master it." And Cain told Abel his brother. And it came about when they were in the field, that Cain rose up against Abel his brother and killed him. Then the LORD said to Cain, "Where is Abel your brother?" And he said, "I do not know. Am I my brother's keeper?" (Genesis 4:5-9 NASB).

There is a very interesting comment made in verse 8. It says, "And Cain told Abel his brother." What did he tell him? After reviewing a large number of Bible commentaries, I could find no one who would make a comment on this particular phrase. After studying this passage for several years, I have come to the opinion that "And Cain told Abel his brother," was descriptive of a family argument. I think that Cain and Abel had words with each other while standing in a field. I think that the discussion got out-of-hand.

Cain had been holding in a great deal of jealousy, bitterness, and hurt. I think he finally let it all out. My guess is that in the process of Cain dumping his feelings, Abel did not appreciate it. He probably said something defensive or unkind back to Cain. I believe that Cain had built up a great deal of resentment. It was in the heat of this argument that Cain struck out in rage and killed his brother. He unleashed his pent-up anger and hatred.

Why do people act the way they do? Why do you act the way you do? Why are some people easier to get along with than others? Part of the answer lies in understanding a person's personality and social style.

Some people are more extroverted, outgoing, assertive, and telling in their behaviors. Others are more introverted, quiet, less assertive, and asking in their actions.

There are those who become quite involved in tasks. To them, life and excitement are found in activities. On the other hand, some people find their fulfillment in relationships with people. Tasks are a low priority for them.

In the following diagram I have listed four basic social styles that are descriptive of how people act: Analytical, Driver, Amiable, and Expressive.

- Analyticals are task-oriented and more asking.
- Drivers are task-oriented and more telling.
- Amiables are relationship-oriented and more asking.
- Expressives are relationship-oriented and more telling.

When under pressure, the four social styles react differently. They all handle the daily stress of life in their own unique way. When the four social styles

Primary Social Style

TASK

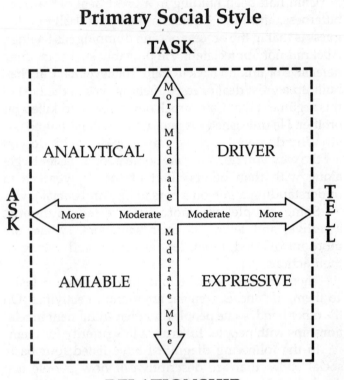

ANALYTICAL		DRIVER
AMIABLE		EXPRESSIVE

(More Moderate / Moderate More — ASK ← → TELL)

RELATIONSHIP

have their "back-against-the-wall" they will respond with negative behavior.

The root response or basic reaction for the Analyticals and Amiables is that of fear. Analyticals will usually tend to become less assertive. They will control their emotions. They will hold in their feelings, keep quiet, and not share their ideas. They will try to avoid, dodge, escape, and retreat from other people or undesirable situations. They have strong withdrawal tendencies. Their silence is almost deafening.

The response to stress is similar for the Amiables.

They, too, will withdraw. But their withdrawal is just a little different. They will withdraw to try to save the relationship. They will tend to give in to other people to keep the peace and reduce conflict. They may appear to even agree with others but are in disagreement inside their mind. They will try to save relationships even if they are the ones who get hurt the most. Although they talk more, it is difficult to get to the bottom of their true thoughts and feelings.

Drivers and Expressives respond to stress and conflict with the strong basic emotion of anger. When faced with a situation that is not going the way they would like it to, the Drivers will become dogmatic. They will tend to be overassertive, autocratic, and unbending. They will often overcontrol the situation. They will attempt to impose their thoughts and feelings on others. The Drivers will literally drive people away.

Expressives will also become very vocal. They have a tendency to attack others and their ideas. They will use condemnation and put-downs and will attempt to discredit the thoughts of others. They have strong emotions and will not slow down in telling others how they feel about things. Expressives usually do not get ulcers. More often they are "carriers." They *give* ulcers.

When the four social styles respond with back-against-the-wall behavior, conflict between people is the result. This is not to say that the various social styles do not have positive behavior. They certainly do. The following chart lists their strengths as well as their weaknesses.

To help you identify your social style and the social style of your family, friends, and fellow workers, ask yourself a few questions. Am I an asker or a teller? Is my first reaction to share my ideas and thoughts or to hold them in?

Strengths and Weaknesses

Analyticals

Negative	Positive
Moody	Industrious
Critical	Gifted
Negative	Perfectionistic
Rigid	Persistent
Indecisive	Conscientious
Legalistic	Loyal
Self-centered	Serious
Stuffy	Aesthetic
Touchy	Idealistic
Vengeful	Exacting
Picky	Sensitive
Persecution-	Self-sacrificing
prone	Orderly
Unsociable	Self-
Moralistic	disciplined
Theoretical	

Drivers

Negative	Positive
Unsympa-	Determined
thetic	Independent
Pushy	Productive
Insensitive	Strong-willed
Inconsiderate	Visionary
Severe	Optimistic
Hostile	Active
Sarcastic	Practical
Tough	Courageous
Unforgiving	Decisive
Domineering	Self-confident
Opinionated	Efficient
Prejudiced	Leader
Harsh	
Proud	

Negative	Positive
Unbothered	Calm
Conforming	Supportive
Blasé	Easygoing
Indolent	Likable
Unsure	Respectful
Spectator	Diplomatic
Selfish	Efficient
Ingratiating	Willing
Stingy	Organized
Stubborn	Conservative
Dependent	Practical
Self-protective	Dependable
Indecisive	Reluctant
Awkward	leader
Fearful	Agreeable
	Dry-humored

Negative	Positive
Weak-willed	Outgoing
Manipulative	Ambitious
Restless	Charismatic
Disorganized	Warm
Unproductive	Stimulating
Excitable	Responsive
Undependable	Talkative
Undisciplined	Enthusiastic
Obnoxious	Carefree
Loud	Compassionate
Reactive	Dramatic
Exaggerating	Generous
Fearful	Friendly
Egotistical	

Amiables

Expressives

GENERAL OVERVIEW OF THE FOUR SOCIAL STYLES

AREA	ANALYTICALS	DRIVERS	AMIABLES	EXPRESSIVE
Reaction	Slow	Swift	Unhurried	Rapid
Orientation	Thinking and fact	Action and goal	Relationship and peace	Involvement and intuition
Likes	Organization	To be in charge	Close relationships	Much interaction
Dislikes	Involvement	Inaction	Conflict	To be alone
Maximum effort	To organize	To control	To relate	To involve
Minimum concern	For relationships	For caution in relationships	For effecting change	For routine
Behavior directed toward achievement	Works carefully and alone— primary effort	Works quickly and alone— primary effort	Works slowly and with others— secondary effort	Works quickly and with team— secondary effort
Behavior directed toward acceptance	Impress others with precision and knowledge— secondary effort	Impress others with individual effort— secondary effort	Gets along as integral member of group— primary effort	Gets along as exciting member of group— primary effort
Actions	Cautious	Decisive	Slow	Impulsive
Skills	Good problem-solving skills	Good administrative skills	Good counseling skills	Good persuasive skills
Decision-making	Avoids risks, based on facts	Takes risks, based on intuition	Avoids risks, based on opinion	Takes risks, based on hunches
Time frame	Historical	Present	Present	Future
Use of time	Slow, deliberate, disciplined	Swift, efficient, impatient	Slow, calm, undisciplined	Rapid, quick, undisciplined

Next, determine if you are more task-oriented, or relationship-oriented. Would your first preference be to work with people, or with ideas and things?

I know what you are going to say: "Sometimes I share my feelings and sometimes I don't. Sometimes I work with people and sometimes I don't." Yes, that is true. However, what do you do in *most* situations? What is your *usual* response? What would your family and friends say was your *most common* reaction? Be honest.

Let's illustrate this concept by looking at four former presidents. How would you rate the following?

President	Asker	Teller	Task	Relationship
Richard Nixon	❏	❏	❏	❏
Jimmy Carter	❏	❏	❏	❏
Ronald Reagan	❏	❏	❏	❏
Woodrow Wilson	❏	❏	❏	❏

President Nixon would be the Driver, President Carter would be the Amiable, President Reagan would be the Expressive, and President Wilson would be the Analytical.

Part of what creates tension between people is that everyone sees life from a different perspective. You probably remember the story of the four blind men who got lost in the jungle. They were all holding hands and trying to get back to their camp, when they ran into an elephant who was munching on some grass.

The first blind man reached out his hand and grabbed the elephant's tail. "It feels like some kind of brush," he announced.

The second man bumped his nose on the elephant's side. "It feels like a wall to me," he said.

The third blind man stumbled into the elephant's

front leg. He wrapped both of his arms around the leg and said, "You're both wrong. It is a large tree."

The last man was groping in the air when his hands felt the elephant's trunk. He leaped back and yelled, "I've grabbed a snake."

The Analyticals and Amiables are more deductive and methodical in their thinking process. Drivers and Expressives are more intuitive and immediate.

This creates stress because the Drivers and Expressives are faster-paced than the Analyticals and Amiables. Neither group has patience for those who differ from their viewpoint.

The Analyticals and Amiables think the Drivers and Expressives are rash in their behavior and thinking. The Drivers and Expressives wonder if the Analyticals and Amiables will ever make a decision in their lives.

It is important for us to be reminded that everyone is unique. We don't all look at things the same way. We need to accept the fact that everyone will not react the same way in a given situation.

Let's Go Out to Dinner!

If the four social styles went out to dinner together, what might happen? The Driver might ask, "Where would you like to go to eat?" "Oh, anywhere," responds the Analytical.

"How about Chinese tonight?"

"No, I don't think so."

"How about a hamburger?"

"Well, that's not what I am hungry for."

"Then you decide."

"No, you choose the place."

"I know a great Mexican restaurant."

"Not tonight. I had Mexican food for lunch."

"It sounds like you have a definite opinion of what you want. Where do you want to go?"

"I don't care. You choose the place."

Finally the Driver makes a decision out of sheer frustration. When they arrive and the waitress comes to the table, who is the first to be ready to order? The Driver, of course. What is happening to the Analytical? He can't make up his mind. There are too many choices. The Amiable hasn't decided because he wants to know what everyone else is going to get. He wouldn't want to choose something that would be too different from the rest of the group. The Expressive is not ready to order either. He hasn't even looked at the menu. He is too involved in talking to strangers at another table.

The different ways people think, and their fast or slow pace, causes them to rub each other raw in relationships. Patience runs thin. Tempers have a tendency to flair. Angry words are spoken. Hurt feelings are created, and trouble is born.

Along with the fast pace versus slow pace problem, comes a difference in priorities. The first priority for Analyticals and Drivers is to accomplish tasks. It is in the doing of things that their self-image is formed. If they are not involved with some goal or purpose, they become frustrated, irritable, and depressed.

When Analyticals and Drivers have to deal with people for a long period of time, they have a tendency to run out of gas. They don't feel good. They begin to run over people and cease to display kindness. To get revived, they need to pull into the filling station of solitude and tasks. They will regain their energy by getting away from people for a while and accomplishing some task. This gives them the strength to again work with people.

Amiables and Expressives are just the opposite.

Their first priority is relationships with people. If they have to deal with facts, details, and tasks, they run out of gas. Being with people and talking with people gives them the pep to do the thing they hate the most: tasks. Their self-image is formed from how they deal with people. Task-oriented people and relationship-oriented people have a hard time understanding each other. The Analyticals and Drivers think that Amiables and Expressives don't care about tasks. Amiables and Expressives do not think that Analyticals and Drivers care about people.

Have you ever wondered why you have a more difficult time with some people rather than with others? It is most likely because they are a criss-cross to your social style. You experience both pace and priority problems with them.

Analyticals have the hardest time with Expressive people who are disorganized and impulsive. Expressives struggle with Analyticals and all of their uptight details.

Drivers have no patience for the Amiable who never can make a decision and is slow as a snail. Amiables have no respect for the Driver who is pushy, demanding, and insensitive. They think that the Driver just steamrolls over people.

The chart on the following page is a general overview of the differences between the four social styles.

Nobody cares how much you know—
until they know how much you care.
—John Cassis

What does all this knowledge about social styles do for us? It helps us to understand others. Once we

Pace and Priority Problems

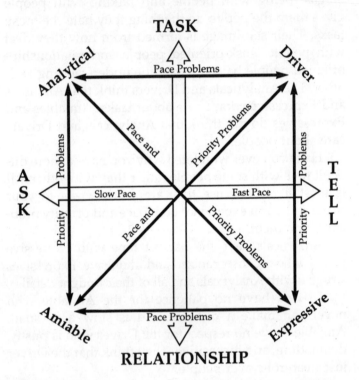

see that other people think differently and react differently than we do, we can begin to develop tolerance.

We can become responsible people by being patient and slowing down our pace, or speeding up our pace to be a peacemaker rather than a hostile person. If we understand that our mates and children have different priorities than we do, it helps us to learn how to deal with them on their level.

Are you a demanding, perfectionist Analytical, who has a free-spirited mate or child? Are you an

Expressive who never finishes the jobs you start, or is always late for appointments, and drives the family crazy? Are you the demanding Driver who is never wrong and has a very sensitive son or daughter who desperately tries to please you? Are you an Amiable who avoids responsibilities because you hate any kind of conflict? You would rather go through a divorce than deal with difficulties.[1]

Many of the relationship problems that you are now experiencing would disappear if you would change how you respond to others. You have been waiting too long for others to change their behaviors. They will change their actions if you change yours. (Isn't it funny how we all wait for the other person to make the first move?)

What I am talking about is reaching out to others with love. The basis for getting along with people is found in the words of Jesus Christ. One day a religious leader approached Jesus and asked Him to identify the greatest commandment in the Law. Jesus replied:

> Love "the LORD your God with all your heart and with all your soul and with all your mind." This is the first and greatest commandment. And the second is like it: "Love your neighbor as yourself." All the Law and the Prophets hang on these two commandments (Matthew 22:37-40 NIV).

> Love is very patient and kind, never jealous or envious, never boastful or proud, never haughty or selfish or rude. Love does not demand its own way. It is not irritable or touchy. It does not hold grudges and will hardly even notice when others do it wrong.

It is never glad about injustice, but rejoices whenever truth wins out. If you love someone you will be loyal to him no matter what the cost. You will always believe in him, always expect the best of him, and always stand your ground in defending him. . . . There are three things that remain—faith, hope, and love—and the greatest of these is love (1 Corinthians 13:4-7,13).

Dear God,

There are some people in my life who rub me the wrong way. I find that when I am around them for a while, I become irritated. They do things so differently than I do. They march to a different drummer.

Help me learn to understand them. Help me realize that they may think and respond differently than I do. Help me appreciate our differences in pace and priorities.

I need to learn patience. I need to learn tolerance. I need to become less selfish. There are some people who I have a hard time loving. Please help me put my love thoughts into action. This is a big order, but I need to start somewhere. Thank You for bringing these people into my life so that I might grow and mature.

Locating Your Family

On the social style grid below, place your name in the appropriate box. Next, place the first names of your family members in their area of social style strength.

This mapping will help you to become aware of your family's social styles, their back-against-the-wall tendencies, areas of possible conflict, and your need to adjust your behavior to better reach out to them in love.

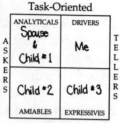

Task-Oriented

	ANALYTICALS	DRIVERS	
A S K E R S	Spouse & Child #1	Me	T E L L E R S
	Child #2	Child #3	
	AMIABLES	EXPRESSIVES	

Relationship-Oriented

Example

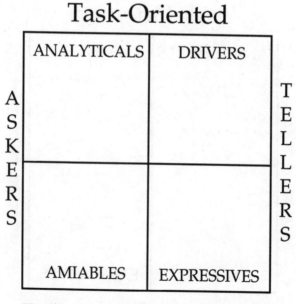

Task-Oriented

	ANALYTICALS	DRIVERS	
A S K E R S			T E L L E R S
	AMIABLES	EXPRESSIVES	

Relationship-Oriented

Locating Your Friends

On the social style grid below, place your name in the appropriate box. Next, place the first names of your friends in their area of social style strength.

This mapping will help you to become aware of your friends' social styles, their back-against-the-wall tendencies, areas of possible conflict, and your need to adjust your behavior to better reach out to them in love.

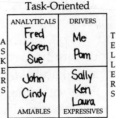

Task-Oriented

ANALYTICALS	DRIVERS
Fred	Me
Karen	Pam
Sue	
John	Sally
Cindy	Ken
	Laura
AMIABLES	EXPRESSIVES

A S K E R S (left) · T E L L E R S (right)

Relationship-Oriented

Example

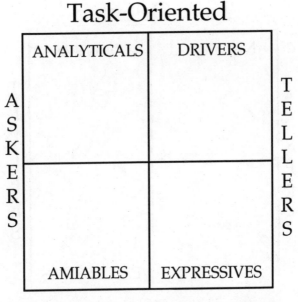

Task-Oriented

ANALYTICALS	DRIVERS
AMIABLES	EXPRESSIVES

A S K E R S (left) · T E L L E R S (right)

Relationship-Oriented

Locating Your Fellow Workers

On the social style grid below, place your name in the appropriate box. Next, place the first names of your fellow workers in their area of social style strength.

This mapping will help you to become aware of your fellow workers' social styles, their back-against-the-wall tendencies, areas of possible conflict, and your need to adjust your behavior to better reach out to them in love.

Task-Oriented

	ANALYTICALS	DRIVERS	
A S K E R S	Gary	Me	T E L L E R S
	Julie	Bob	
	Janet	Carl	
	Jeff	Lisa	
	AMIABLES	EXPRESSIVES	

Relationship-Oriented

Example

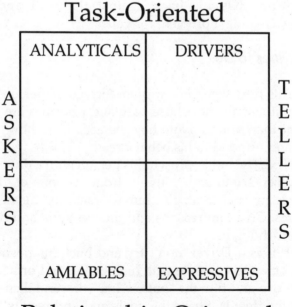

Task-Oriented

	ANALYTICALS	DRIVERS	
A S K E R S			T E L L E R S
	AMIABLES	EXPRESSIVES	

Relationship-Oriented

Discussion Questions

1. What type of social style is the hardest for you to deal with?

2. What are the negative traits of your social style that need to be changed?

3. What are some practical steps that you can practice to learn patience?

4. Ask three people who know you to give their opinion of what social style they think you are. Do these match your viewpoint? Do you need to have a new look at the way you come across to others?

5. What response should you have when someone has his back against the wall and is creating a problem for you?

Activities to Do

This next week, identify an "irregular person" in your life (someone whose pace and priorities are different than yours). Note how he acts. Note how you feel and respond to his behaviors.

Next, try and approach this person with a different mind-set. Try to look at things from his point of view. If he is an Analytical, give him the facts and details he desires. Give him reasons and time to think and react to new thoughts.

If he is a Driver, don't try and buck his position. Don't try and compete with him. Be fair and firm, and be sure to give him the "bottom line" first and then discuss the details. Share the goals and end results that you would like to see.

If he is an Amiable, calm his fears or concerns. Reaffirm your relationship with him. Provide direction, instruction, and encouragement. Work alongside him as a partner.

If he is an Expressive, don't be overcome by his strong opinions. Create a climate of excitement, enthusiasm, and friendship. Give him endorsement and encouragement.

Now keep up your new way of responding to this "irregular person." After a couple of weeks, take a new look at your relationship. Has it become a little less troublesome? Has tension gone down between you? Have you felt a little more at ease? Maybe there is hope after all.

Verses to Look Up

Deuteronomy 10:12
Matthew 22:37-40
John 13:34,35
John 14:21-24
Romans 12:9,10

Galatians 5:22,23
1 Thessalonians 3:12
1 Peter 1:22
1 John 3:14
1 John 4:11,19,21

CHAPTER TEN

Forgiveness—the Hardest Thing to Do

> *He that cannot forgive others breaks the bridge over which he must pass himself; for every man has need to be forgiven.*

> —*Thomas Fuller*

"How could he do such a thing? How could he take my money and other people's money and just throw it away?" It was easy to see that Richard was not a happy man. He had invested his life savings in a real estate deal with a friend. When the recession hit, the housing market began to collapse. Richard's friend had overextended his credit and was building on borrowed money. When the bank wanted payment, no money was available. The limited partnership went into bankruptcy.

"That dirty dog has ruined my future. All of my retirement money is gone. I'd like to punch his lights out. It will be a cold day in the hot place before I'd ever forgive him."

Everyone has experienced some form of personal, financial, or social hurt. Have you ever had a friend let you down or disappoint you? Have you experienced difficulties with one or more of your relatives? Have your boyfriend or girlfriend or spouse ever said or done something to really hurt you? Have your children caused you a great deal of pain? Have you become disgusted with someone at work?

Have you been involved in an accident that wasn't your fault but cost you a great deal of money? Has a drunk driver taken the life of a loved one? Did someone you love recently die? Do you have a family member who is very sick? Have you ever been mad at God? Have you been upset over all the injustice in the world? Have you been struggling with the concept of forgiveness?

Cain had to deal with these issues. He felt that he had been dealt with unfairly. He became jealous and harbored resentment against his brother Abel. Cain carried a grudge, nursed it, and watered it with thoughts of revenge. He let the plant of bitterness and hatred grow until it produced the fruit of premeditated murder.

In Genesis 4:9, God asked Cain where his brother was. This question came not because God didn't know the answer. God knew that Abel had been killed. He was asking Cain so that he would have to face the issue (his sin) and deal with it.

I am sure that Cain looked in all directions before he murdered Abel. He didn't want any witnesses. He forgot to look one direction. He forgot to look up. We do the same thing, don't we? We think that no one knows what we have done, that it is hidden. Except, like Cain, we forget to look up. God knows all of our actions. He even knows what we are thinking.

God knows about the person toward whom you are holding hatred and resentment. Oh, you may hide it from the outside world. Your friends may not be aware. Your spouse may not know. But God is fully aware.

Dr. S. I. McMillen in his book *None of These Diseases* illustrates what happens when we harbor resentment. When we hold on to thoughts of revenge, we begin to die inside:

> The moment I start hating a man, I become his slave. I can't enjoy my work anymore because he even controls my thoughts. My resentments produce too many stress hormones in my body and I become fatigued after only a few hours of work. The work I formerly enjoyed is now drudgery. Even vacations cease to give me pleasure. It may be a luxurious car that I drive along the lake fringed with the autumnal beauty of maple, oak and birch. As far as my experience of pleasure is concerned, I might as well be driving a wagon in mud and rain.
>
> The man I hate hounds me wherever I go. I can't escape his tyrannical grasp on my mind. When the waiter serves me porterhouse steak with French fries, asparagus, crisp salad, and strawberry shortcake smothered with ice cream, it might as well be stale bread and water. My teeth chew the food and I swallow it, but the man I hate will not permit me to enjoy it.
>
> The man I hate may be many miles from my bedroom; but more cruel than any slave driver, he whips my thoughts into such a frenzy that my innerspring mattress becomes a rack of torture. The lowliest of the serfs can sleep, but not I. I really must acknowledge the fact that I am a slave to every man on whom I pour the vials of my wrath.[1]

Has this been your experience? Is there someone in your life who you need to forgive? Have you been hanging on to hatred? Have you wanted revenge? Have you longed for repayment? Have you, like Cain, been holding resentment?

Then just let go of it. "But you don't understand, Bob! It's not fair what they have done to me. They have hurt me for years. They don't seem to care. I can't forgive them."

Can't or won't?

Let me ask you this: Has your current behavior been working? I mean, are you at peace? Do you have joy in your heart? Has holding on to all the resentment helped your situation? How long are you going to go on having your insides eaten out thinking about this problem? Wouldn't you like some relief? Wouldn't you like to get rid of this burden?

Then forgive. You won't be happy or find peace until you do. It has been my experience that people will try to do anything rather than forgive. They will participate in heavy physical workout sessions and run for miles. They will go to therapy sessions and share all of their frustrations and angers with their counselor. They will pay thousands of dollars in medical bills and take bushels of pills. They will read book after book searching for an answer to the hurts of life. They may even choose to act crazy. They will do anything rather than forgive.

You see, the reason that forgiveness is so difficult is because the person who is the injured party does the forgiving. The person who caused the injury goes free.

Forgiveness is the fragrance the violet sheds
on the heel that has crushed it.
—*Mark Twain*

At the turn of the century the great preacher Henry Ward Beecher said, "If you haven't forgotten an offense toward you, you haven't truly forgiven it." Have you heard comments similar to that? I am sure you have. Do you know what that statement is? It is a lie. We never forget. We always remember.

Forgiveness does not reside in forgetting. Forgiveness is not a feeling. Forgiveness simply lets the offending party go free.

Let's say that I came over to your house for a visit. Upon entering, I am carrying a coat over my shoulder. As I turn, the coat happens to hit a priceless heirloom vase that has been in your family for generations. The coat knocks it off the stand and it starts to fall.

We both lunge for the vase but are too late. The vase hits the tile and breaks into hundreds of pieces. I feel terrible. You are in shock. The whole situation is a disaster.

I turn to you and say, "I'm sorry. Can I buy you another one?"

"No," you groan.

"Can I replace it?"

"No." Your heart is breaking.

"Will you forgive me?"

Inside you groan even more.

You see, that's the problem. There is no way the offending party can repay you for the hurt he caused. If you decided to get revenge and break one of the vases at my house, it would be a hollow victory. You would have dropped to the same level, and still you wouldn't have a restored vase. You might just decide to hold resentment toward me for breaking your vase. Then who hurts? I will soon forget about the vase and go my way. But you will not only have a broken vase, you will also be stewing in your own caldron of hatred.

You will not only have the original hurt, but you will also have daily and continual hurt as you replay the event over and over again. It is not a pretty picture. David Augsburger says it this way: "Forgiveness is surrendering my right to hurt you back if you hurt me."

If forgiveness isn't a feeling, what is it? If I don't really forget hurtful events, how do I forgive? Dr. Jay Adams suggests that forgiveness is not a feeling but a promise or commitment. It is a promise or commitment to three things:

1. I will not use the event against them in the future.

2. I will not talk to others about them.

3. I will not dwell on it myself.

I know that is a tough assignment. You may not be ready for it. You may want to try the resentment method for a little while longer. God is patient. He will wait for you to come to the end of your way. He will be there to help you learn to forgive when you finally let go of the bitterness.

The grease of forgiving love can reduce the friction and salve the irritation. Forgiveness is not holy amnesia which erases the past—instead it is the experience of healing that draws the poison out. You may recall that hurt but you will not relive the hurt. The hornet of memory may fly again, but forgiveness has drawn out the sting.
—David Augsburger

This is the "second-mile concept" that Jesus talked about when He said,

> If the military demand that you carry their gear for a mile, carry it two. Give to those who ask, and don't turn away from those who want to borrow. There is a saying, "Love your friends and hate your enemies." But I say: Love your enemies! Pray for those who persecute you! In that way you will be acting as true sons of your Father in heaven. For he gives his sunlight to both the evil and the good, and sends rain on the just and the unjust too. If you love only those who love you, what good is that? Even scoundrels do that much. If you are friendly only to your friends, how are you different from anyone else? Even the heathen do that. But you are to be perfect, even as your Father in heaven is perfect (Matthew 5:41-48).

All My Children

There is much talk today about dysfunctional families. It is as if we are trying to excuse our present behavior and lay all of the blame for our actions on the shoulders of our parents. Have you ever wondered if your children are going to do the same thing to you that you are doing to your parents?

We have all types of support groups for dysfunctional people: Adult Children of Alcoholics, Adult Children of Drug Addicts, Adult Children of Abuse, and the list goes on and on. Wouldn't it be refreshing to start a new support group called Adult Children of Normal Parents? That would be a first.

Why is it that two people can come from the same dysfunctional family and one of them turns out great and the other is a disaster? When we see the child who is a disaster, we say that it's the parents' fault. Now, wait a minute. What about the other child? He is doing fine. He came from the same dysfunctional family. Are we now going to say that he is turning out fine because of the influence of the parents? Not usually. Everyone says in that case, "He turned out great in spite of his parents."

Let's take a look at the family line of Joseph in the Old Testament. It is a classic example of someone who turned out great even coming out of a "dysfunctional family."

We will start with Abraham and Sarai (Sarah). Abraham left Haran when he was 75 years of age. On his way to the land of promise, the Egyptians saw Sarai, Abraham's wife. She was a "knockout," a real beauty. The king was attracted to her. Abraham lied and told the king that Sarai was his sister. It was a half-lie. She was his half-sister.

Later a civil war broke out between Abraham and Lot's cattle herders. It became a "family feud." Abraham gave in and let Lot have his way. Abraham tried to seek family peace at any cost. Sound familiar so far?

Lot proceeded to get in trouble with some kings. Abraham had to go and rescue Lot. Have you ever played the rescue game?

After many years, Sarai was still barren. To be without a child was viewed by everyone as a curse. She was depressed. Trying to help God out, Sarai talked Abraham into having an affair with her hand-maid named Hagar. Hagar became pregnant and had a child named Ishmael.

Soon Hagar and Sarai became embroiled in a fight. Both of the women were fighting for Abraham's affections. Sarai won, and Hagar was kicked out of the home. Abraham was caught between the two women and tried to bring peace. Have you ever tried the peacemaker game?

In the meantime, Sarai was told by the Lord that she was going to have a baby. Because of her old age, she began to laugh at God in disbelief. Nine months later Isaac was born.

As Isaac grew, animosity was generated between Ishmael and Isaac. There was a lot of sibling rivalry going on. Ishmael became the father of the Arab nations and Isaac the father of the Israelites. This animosity continues to this day. Have you ever been involved with sibling rivalry?

Lot began to covet the "good life" of Sodom. He moved to Sodom and became a leader in the town. However, he struggled with his own moral beliefs and the standards of the homosexuals living in Sodom.

God informed Lot that he was going to destroy the wickedness of Sodom by fire and brimstone. He was told to leave, but he did not leave easily. He had to be taken out of the city by angels. Lot finally departed with his wife and two daughters.

Sorrowing over the worldly things being left behind in Sodom, Lot's wife looked back. She instantly turned into a pillar of salt. After leaving Sodom, Lot became drunk and committed incest with his two daughters. They both became pregnant. Have you ever experienced abuse in your family?

Abraham remarried after the death of Sarai. As he was in the process of dying he made a will and left everything to Isaac. This did not make the firstborn son, Ishmael, happy. Many families have argued over the wills left by parents.

Soon a bride was chosen for Isaac. Her name was Rebekah, and it wasn't long before she gave birth to twins, Esau and Jacob. As the children grew, favoritism was shown by both parents. Isaac favored Esau, and Rebekah favored Jacob. Did you grow up in a family where favoritism was shown?

Sweet, loving Rebekah and Jacob designed a plan to trick Esau out of his birthright. Isaac was blind by now and near death. After Rebekah and Jacob fooled the blind Isaac, he discovered the plan. He became quite upset. However, he was not as upset as Esau. Isaac soon died. Were you raised in a family that used a great deal of manipulation?

Esau wanted to kill Jacob, and Jacob ran for his life. He escaped to his Uncle Laban's house. While there he fell in love with Laban's younger daughter, Rachel. Jacob worked for seven years for the opportunity to marry Rachel.

Laban deceived Jacob on his wedding night and substituted Leah (the older sister) as a wife. Jacob must have been half brain-dead because he didn't realize until the next morning that the woman he slept with was Leah rather than Rachel. (I know of a number of people who have claimed that they married the wrong person.)

Not wanting to rock the boat, and because of his great love for Rachel, Jacob worked another seven years to marry her. Now with two wives the trouble really began! Rachel was barren and Leah had children. Leah used this fact to her advantage. (I've been told that the supreme punishment for bigamy is two mothers-in-law.)

Rachel could not take the embarrassment of being childless. She talked Jacob into having an affair with Bilhah, her handmaid. A baby was born. Not to be outdone, Leah talked Jacob into having an affair with her handmaid, Zilpah.

Soon both Leah and Rachel argued over Leah's son's mandrakes. The mandrakes were given to Rachel so Leah could sleep with Jacob. So far, this family line could hold its own with any soap opera on television today.

It wasn't long before Jacob cheated Laban out of the spotted, striped, and speckled sheep. Of course, Jacob put the spots, stripes, and speckles on the sheep. Laban and his sheepherders were not happy with Jacob. Have you ever experienced troubled working relationships?

Jacob, Rachel, and Leah ran away from Laban. In the process of leaving, Rachel stole her father's idols. Laban pursued the group in search of his idols. I know of relatives who fight with each other even though they are miles apart.

Jacob eventually had 12 sons and one daughter from the four women. The daughter's name was Dinah. Dinah was followed by a man named Shechem. He fell in love with her and raped her. Shechem wanted to marry Dinah. Shechem is the original "night stalker."

When Dinah's brothers found out she was raped, they calmly told Shechem that the only way that Dinah would be allowed to marry him was for him to become circumcised—not only him, but all the men in his city. I don't know what Shechem told the men of the city, but whatever he said convinced them all to be circumcised. That had to have been some sales pitch! On the third day, when all of the men of the city were in pain, Dinah's brothers came into the city and slew all of the men.

Jacob showed favoritism to his son Joseph. He made him a coat that had many colors. The other ten brothers plotted to murder Joseph because of their jealousy. Have you ever hated one of your siblings?

Reuben designed a rescue plot to keep Joseph alive. The brothers threw him in a pit, but Reuben planned to come later and save Joseph so he would look like a good guy in the eyes of Jacob. The plans changed when some Midianites came along. The brothers sold Joseph into slavery. Murder turned into a get-rich-quick scheme. The brothers then made up a lie about the death of Joseph. Soon after the episode with Joseph, Reuben had an incestuous affair with his daughter-in-law, Tamar. This is a classic dysfunctional family system.

Joseph became the slave of a man named Potiphar in Egypt. Potiphar's wife was attracted to Joseph and wanted him to sleep with her. Joseph refused. Being a woman scorned, Potiphar's wife yelled "rape" and accused Joseph of sexual harassment. Joseph was thrown in prison without a trial.

In prison, Joseph interpreted dreams for two men. He asked one of the men to help him get out of prison. The man forgot, and Joseph remained in his cell for a couple more years. When the Pharaoh needed a dream interpreted, Joseph's forgetful friend remembered his old cell mate.

Joseph interpreted the Pharaoh's dreams. As a result he became second in command of all Egypt. After seven years, a famine struck the land where Jacob was living. Joseph's brothers came to Egypt to arrange for food. Joseph recognized his brothers. After he revealed who he was, Joseph's brothers thought he was going to take revenge for what they did to him. They thought he was filled with resentment. They were waiting for repayment and retaliation. That's what they would have done. It never happened.

Why?

Because Joseph forgave them.

Joseph told his brothers,

> "Do not be afraid, for am I in God's place?
> And as for you, you meant evil against me,
> but God meant it for good in order to bring

about this present result, to preserve many people alive. So therefore do not be afraid; I will provide for you and your little ones." So he comforted them and spoke kindly to them (Genesis 50:19-21 NASB).

If anyone had a dysfunctional family background, it was Joseph. Yet in the midst of all the infighting, hostility, and immorality, he remained true to God. He took responsibility for his own behavior and chose to forgive all those who had tried to do him harm. He blessed them and did not curse them. He is a great example of godliness in action in the center of great difficulties and hardships.

Have you been struggling with the issue of forgiveness in your life? Is there someone you need to forgive? Then don't put it off anymore. Don't let another day of inner turmoil go by. Settle the matter today. If you want to be your own counselor, bring the matter to God and let Him deal with it.

> Never pay back evil for evil. Do things in such a way that everyone can see you are honest clear through. Don't quarrel with anyone. Be at peace with everyone, just as much as possible. Dear friends, never avenge yourselves. Leave that to God, for he has said that he will repay those who deserve it. [Don't take the law into your own hands.] Instead, feed your enemy if he is hungry. If he is thirsty give him something to drink and you will be "heaping coals of fire on his head." In other words, he will feel ashamed of himself for what he has done to you. Don't let evil get the upper hand but conquer evil by doing good (Romans 12:17-21).

Be gentle and ready to forgive; never hold
grudges. Remember, the Lord forgave you, so
you must forgive others (Colossians 3:13).

Dear God,

To forgive others is a big order. I don't know how You did it. It is so difficult to forgive someone who has hurt me. I think I want to, but the memory of the event keeps coming back to haunt me. Sometimes I live it over and over.

Help me to drive the hornet of memory away. Please take away his big stinger. Please draw out the poison of bitterness and resentment. Teach me how to think about positive things and let go of the past.

I know that I need to go to some people and ask for forgiveness. I have hurt them. Please give me the courage to do this. Give me the right things to say to help heal their pain.

Thank You for loving me enough to die for me and forgive my sins. Help me to exhibit the same godly and forgiving spirit as Joseph.

Forgiveness Exercise

1. List an event that has been difficult for you—a
   situation in which forgiveness is needed:

   _____

   _____

   _____

   _____

   _____

   _____

   _____

   _____

   _____

2. Who is the individual that you need to forgive?

   _____

   _____

3. List reasons why you have not been able to forgive: _____

   _____

   _____

   _____

   _____

   _____

4. What do you think Jesus would like you to do
   in this particular situation?_____

   _____

   _____

   _____

   _____

   _____

   _____

5. Do you need to ask anyone to forgive you for
   your attitude and actions? What do you think
   Jesus would like you to say to this person?

   _____

   _____

   _____

   _____

   _____

6. Joseph comforted those who had hurt him, and he spoke kindly to them. How could you apply this concept with the person(s) who have hurt you? (Comforting and speaking kindly helps you to forget the offense.) _____

_____

_____

_____

_____

_____

7. Make a list of the people you should pray for:

_____

_____

_____

_____

Verses to Look Up

Proverbs 19:11
Proverbs 25:21,22
Matthew 6:12,14
Mark 11:25
Luke 17:3,4

Luke 23:34
Romans 12:14
1 Corinthians 4:12,13
Ephesians 4:32
1 Peter 3:9

CHAPTER ELEVEN

In Search of Peace

*Lord, thou madest us for thyself, and we can
find no rest till we find rest in thee.*

—St. Augustine

"I just can't seem to get my life together," said Brent as he sat down with a big sigh. "I have read self-help books till they're coming out of my ears. I have visited several counselors, and they don't seem to help. I've even gone to church regularly for the past month. Nothing seems to work. When I pray it seems like my prayers just bounce off the ceiling."

"Maybe they do, Brent," I said.

"What do you mean?"

"Maybe your prayers don't go anywhere because you have never received Christ in your life. Can you remember a time when you've asked Christ to take over your life?"

"I'm not sure I know what you mean."

I think that was Cain's problem also. He didn't know God in a personal and living way. He had a form of godliness. He knew how to do the religious exercises and talk the religious talk. However, I don't think he allowed God to change his life.

> If you do well, will not your countenance be lifted up? And if you do not do well, sin is crouching at the door; and its desire is for you, but you must master it (Genesis 4:7 NASB).

God warned Cain that danger was lying ahead. He was heading for trouble unless he changed the road he was traveling down. God alerted him to the fact that he had a choice in the matter. Cain refused to listen. He wanted to do his own thing and go his own way. Dear reader, maybe that is why you have been so discouraged during the past months. Maybe you have been doing your own thing, and God has not been a part of your life. Maybe you know about God instead of knowing Him personally.

> And Cain told Abel his brother. And it came about when they were in the field, that Cain rose up against Abel his brother and killed him. Then the LORD said to Cain, "Where is Abel your brother?" And he said, "I do not know. Am I my brother's keeper?" And He said, "What have you done? The voice of your brother's blood is crying to Me from the ground. And now are you cursed from the ground, which has opened its mouth to receive your brother's blood from your hand. When you cultivate the ground, it shall no longer yield its strength to you; you shall be a vagrant and a wanderer on the earth" (Genesis 4:8-12 NASB).

In the verses above we see that Cain murdered his brother. When God confronted him with his sinful condition, Cain attempted to deny responsibility and change the subject. He did not want to admit the fact that he was a sinner in need of salvation. God proceeded to inform Cain that the ground would not produce for him. There would be no fruit. There would be no joy. There would be no peace. Cain would begin to wander as a result of his actions. Have you been wandering for a long time? Are you in need of peace and joy?

Poisoned Meat and Yellow Butter

In order for you to enjoy a daily peace and joy in your life, you must first experience peace with God. This is done by personally inviting Jesus Christ to come and live in your life. This is an act of faith.

Many people believe *faith* is just a religious word. This is not true. We live our entire lives by faith. We have faith that the butcher won't sell us poisoned meat. We have faith that the person driving an oncoming car will stay in his own lane. We have faith that the pharmacist is putting the right pills in our prescription bottle. We have faith that when we turn on the water faucet water will come out instead of orange juice. Our life on this planet is lived by faith. In many cases, it is blind faith.

I have encountered people who have said, "I will never believe in Christ because I don't understand all there is to know about God." You don't have to know everything about God to have a personal experience with Christ. Do you understand all there is to know about how a black-and-white cow can eat green grass and turn it into white milk and yellow butter? Yet you can enjoy the end result even though you don't understand the process.

Over the years, I have dealt with many people who have had an intellectual encounter with Christ. They know truths about Him. Some even get a little emotional about the teachings of Jesus. Yet they have never personally received Christ.

Are You Married?

If I were to ask you if you knew Christ as your personal Savior, what would you say? "I hope so," or "I think so," or "I'm trying"?

When someone answers with a shade of doubt, I often say, "Ask me if I am married."

This usually takes them a little off guard. They say, "What?"

"Ask me if I am married."

"Are you married?"

"I hope so. I think so. I'm trying."

No, my friend, when you are married, you know so! When you receive Christ, there is no doubt. You know so!

Have you received Christ by faith? Do you know that your sins are forgiven? Can you remember a time when you made this commitment?

If not, you probably do not know Christ. This may be why you can't seem to get your life together. But you are not alone in this situation. I have met many people who only have a head knowledge and not a heart knowledge of Christ.

As I look back on my life, I can see that I grew up in a Bible-believing church but still only had a head knowledge of Jesus. I cannot remember a time that I didn't believe in Jesus—that He was the Son of God who died for my sins However, it wasn't until I was around 20 years of age that I realized the need to personally invite Christ into my life.

Could you be in the same situation? If so, how about making that decision right now? You do not have to bow your head. You can make this decision with your eyes wide open.

In Romans 10:9,10 we read,

> For if you tell others with your own mouth that Jesus Christ is your LORD, and believe in your own heart that God has raised him from the dead, you will be saved. For it is by believing in his heart that a man becomes right with God; and with his mouth he tells others of his faith, confirming his salvation.

Are you willing to tell others that Jesus is your Lord? Do you believe God raised Jesus from the dead? If so, then you are saved according to the Word of God.

Faith Is More Than Feelings

You may say, "But I don't feel any different." Feelings do not count at this point. The important thing is an act of your will by faith. The feelings will come later. The following chart will help to illustrate this:

1. HEAR—FACTS—MIND

2. BELIEVE ⎱
3. RECEIVE ⎰ FAITH—EMOTIONS

4. DO—FEELINGS—WILL

Often people become involved with numbers 1 and 2 and not with 3 and 4. There are two parts to true faith. I could show you a real 1000-dollar bill and tell you I was going to give it to you (number 1). You could even believe it was real (number 2), and still not be in ownership of it. It is only when you mix your belief and faith and receive it that it becomes yours (number 3). Then the feelings will come (number 4).

I have had people tell me, "If I could only feel the way you do about God, then I would believe." That is putting the cart before the horse. That would be like saying, "If I could feel like I owned 1000 dollars, then I would believe it." No, first comes the twofold step of faith.

Often individuals are plagued with doubt about their decision for Christ. They have not felt any real assurance that they are saved. This is usually because they are told by others that they should have some great emotional experience. To most people, this does not happen. When they read stories or hear of other people who have some "gigantic spiritual goose pimple," they feel left out. They wonder if they are second-class Christians.

Satan is deceiving many people today with that type of thinking. There is no "instant spirituality." There is no "special gift" that will set you on a higher spiritual plane. God has placed us in Christ as joint heirs by an act of simple, childlike faith. It is as simple as that, and man cannot add to or take away from that fact.

What God Says

Listen to what God Himself says about the security that is yours in Christ Jesus, and then claim these promises for yourself:

> God has said, "I will never, never fail you nor forsake you" (Hebrews 13:5).

> And what is it that God has said? That he has given us eternal life, and that this life is in his Son. So whoever has God's Son has life; whoever does not have his Son, does not have life. I have written this to you who believe in the Son of God so that you may know you have eternal life (1 John 5:11-13).

Jesus Himself declared:

> My sheep recognize my voice, and I know them, and they follow me. I give them eternal life and they shall never perish. No one shall snatch them away from me, for my Father has given them to me, and he is more powerful than anyone else, so no one can kidnap them from me. I and the Father are one (John 10:27-30).

Wouldn't it be good if today, by faith, you would settle the issue of your salvation? Invite Christ into your life and seal your decision by claiming God's assurance. Then determine with God's help not to return to your old life and your old way of thinking.

The following may help you to understand what I have been talking about.

The Dynamic Life

Is it possible to experience joy, peace, and happiness and to have a dynamic life?

Dynamic living is only found in a personal relationship with God . . . made possible by Jesus Christ.

Jesus told him, "I am the Way—yes, and the Truth and the Life. No one can get to the Father except by means of me" (John 14:6).

I came that they might have life, and might have it abundantly (John 10:10 NASB).

To understand this concept, let's take a look at man's beginning in the Garden of Eden.

God created man in His own image (Genesis 1:27 NASB).

The "image" of God refers to man's mind, will, and emotions.

SPIRIT
God-consciousness or awareness (Job 32:8; Psalm 18:28; Proverbs 20:27).

SOUL
Heart of man . . . man's mind, will, emotions (Genesis 2:7; Psalm 13:2; 1 Thessalonians 5:23; Hebrews 4:12).

BODY
Physical body . . . the five senses (Genesis 1:26).

In the beginning God and man had perfect fellowship (relationship).

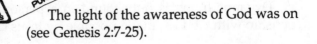

The light of the awareness of God was on (see Genesis 2:7-25).

Man disobeyed and his relationship with God was broken (Genesis 2:17; 31-24).

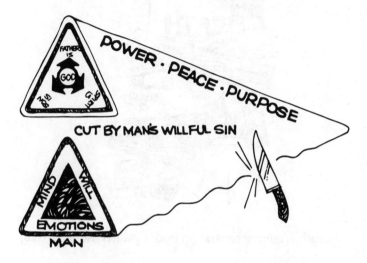

The spirit of man died toward God. . . . The light was put out (see Ephesians 4:18).

God does not force us to love Him . . . the choice is ours.

Man chose to disbobey God. The disobedience was sin.

When Adam sinned, sin entered the entire human race. His sin spread death throughout all the world, so everything began to grow old and die, for all sinned (Romans 5:12).

For all have sinned, and come short of the glory of God (Romans 3:23 KJV).

THE WAGE OF SIN IS

Death is eternal separation from God (see Romans 6:23).

WHAT IS THE REMEDY?

Jesus is the only way back to God (see John 14:6).

Jesus restores the relationship
(Romans 5:8; Hebrews 9:15;
1 Timothy 2:5; 1 Peter 3:18).

Would you like to experience a dynamic life? Would you like to receive Jesus?

You can by a simple prayer of faith. Remember that becoming a Christian is not just saying words. It's receiving a person—Jesus.

> Dear Lord Jesus,
>   I would like to receive You into my life. Thank You for dying in my place. Thank You for pardoning my sins. Thank You for the gift of eternal life. Help me, by Your Holy Spirit, to live for You.
>
>   Amen

When someone becomes a Christian he becomes a brand new person inside. He is not the same any more. A new life has begun! (2 Corinthians 5:17).

To help you in this dynamic life, Jesus must be the controller of your life.

Jesus wants to reinvade your mind, will, and emotions and establish His control.

How do we apply God's remedy?

**RECEIVE
JESUS
INTO YOUR
HEART
BY FAITH**

FREE GIFT-
Romans 6:23;
Ephesians 2:8,9

But to all who received him, he gave the right to become children of God. All they needed to do was to trust him to save them (John 1:12).

What happens when one receives Jesus into his life?

**GOD BY HIS
HOLY SPIRIT
ENTERS
OUR LIFE**

God again turns on the light of God-consciousness or awareness in the spirit of man (see Titus 3:5,6).

Dear God,

I want to come before You today and thank You for sending Christ to die for my sins. Thank You that Jesus rose from the dead that I may have eternal life. I want You to come into my life and save me.

I know that I need You to help me as I face life's pressures. I know that You want to bring me support and courage. Thank You for caring about the smallest details of my life.

Help me this day to live a godly life for You. May my life be an example and help to others. Help me to realize that You are the Great Counselor. You created me and know how I function best. Help me to get into Your Word so that I may grow and mature as a Christian.

Growth Helps

1. Thank God for your new relationship with Him. Look up the following verses: Revelation 3:20; Colossians 1:14,27; 1 John 5:11-13; John 6:37; Romans 10:9-13; and Hebrews 13:5. What did you learn from these verses? _____

   _____

   _____

   _____

   _____

   _____

2. Read the Bible every day. Following is a very simple daily Bible study plan.

   A. Select one of the books within the Bible that you would like to read.

   B. Read one chapter a day until you are finished with that book.

    C. As you read each chapter make some notes. Try and identify the following:

        1. The key verse of the chapter.

        2. God's commands. (A command is something to do.)

        3. God's promises. (A promise is something to be believed.)

        4. A summary of the chapter.

        5. Personal applications that you received from reading that particular chapter.

    D. Look up 1 Peter 2:2 and Psalm 119:9,11.

3. Talk to God daily and keep your relationship with Him growing. Read: 1 John 1:9; Psalm 66:18; and Philippians 4:6,7.

4. Fellowship with other believers. Get involved in a church where Christ is preached (see Hebrews 10:25).

5. Begin to tell others about Jesus. Learn to serve God wherever you can. Help other Christians grow in their faith. Look up Matthew 28:19,20; Mark 5:19; Acts 1:8; Ephesians 4:29; and 1 Corinthians 10:31. What did you learn from reading these Bible verses?_____

_____

_____

_____

_____

_____

_____

_____

_____

CHAPTER TWELVE

Slaying the Giant of Fear

Worry is a thin stream of fear trickling through the mind. If encouraged, it cuts a channel into which all other thoughts are drained.

—*A. S. Roche*

"I get these migraine headaches several times a week. I even miss work because of them," said Sandy as she stiffened in the chair.

"Do you find yourself daydreaming a lot? By that I mean, when you are working at a task, do you catch yourself thinking about something other than the project at hand?"

"All the time. I have a real problem with concentration."

"How long has this been going on?"

"It started about a year ago."

"Did you have any emotional traumas or large hurts in your life about a year ago?"

Sandy's brow furrowed slightly. She then looked down at her lap and sighed. She was quiet for a few seconds. "That was when Don and I first started to have problems. I think he is going to leave me."

"Did he say he was going to leave you?"

"No," she continued. "I just have this nagging feeling that he will. We don't communicate very well."

Fear and worry have a way of clouding the mind. The more you think about a negative situation, the more it seems to grow in your mind. You begin to have imaginary conversations with people who have said or done something to hurt you. You begin to plan your verbal responses. You think about methods and ways to get even. Every free moment your mind returns to the problem you can't seem to get away from. Worry has the ability to give very large shadows to small things.

Have you ever pulled up to a stoplight in your car and turned to look and see who is in the car next to you? Have you smiled to yourself as you have noticed the person next to you talking and having a conversation, and no one else is in the car? Have you seen people walking down the street talking into the air as if someone was next to them? (Maybe you have done it yourself!)

It's okay to talk with yourself. It's okay to answer yourself. It's when you disagree with your answers that you've got a problem.
—R. E. Phillips

How many times do we have imaginary conversations with imaginary people about imaginary situations? Probably more than we would like to admit. Anxiety, fear, and worry can be the causes for many of these conversations. Small molehill problems can begin to grow into large emotional mountains that are difficult to climb.

People are filled with all kinds of fear. Their fears include fear of failure, fear of high places, fear of people, fear of exposure, fear of loss, fear of success, fear of God, and fear of the dark.

I can remember as a child being afraid of the dark. Sometimes I would have to take the trash out at night. We lived on the corner of a block in Denver, Colorado. It was a long walk on the side of the house to the fence gate that led to the backyard. The streetlight on the corner gave a little light. But when I entered the backyard, there was no light. Trees and bushes were on both sides of the yard. I would imagine that people were hiding in them waiting to grab me. Crossing about 60 feet of lawn, I would have to turn at the end of the garage and walk toward the alley. All kinds of people used to walk up and down our alley. I just knew that someone would be hiding behind the garbage cans.

I tried whistling in the dark, pretending that I was not afraid. It did not work. I became more afraid that my whistling would attract the attention of the person hiding in the bushes.

As soon as I would dump the trash in the garbage can, I would run as fast as I could through the backyard, out the gate, and up the side of the house. What a relief it was to get back inside where there was light and I was safe.

Each time I took the trash out, the fear began to grow. Every time I ran back to the house, it was faster and faster. I held the record for night garbage running. Even though no one ever grabbed me in the dark, I always thought someone would.

Worry is faith in the negative, trust in the unpleasant, assurance of disaster, and belief in defeat. Worry is a magnet that attracts negative conditions; faith is a more powerful force that creates positive circumstances. Worry is wasting today's time to clutter up tomorrow's opportunities with yesterday's troubles.
—William A. Ward

Isn't it funny how we spend so much time in fear and worrying about things that never happen? The more we think about a particular fear, the more it grows in our mind. Fear is one of our basic emotions. It is one of the first emotions recorded in the Bible:

> Then the eyes of both of them were opened, and they knew that they were naked; and they sewed fig leaves together and made themselves loin coverings. And they heard the sound of the LORD God walking in the garden in the cool of the day, and the man and his wife hid themselves from the presence of the LORD God among the trees of the garden. Then the LORD God called to the man, and said to him, "Where are you?" And he said, "I heard the sound of Thee in the garden, and I was afraid because I was naked; so I hid myself" (Genesis 3:7-10 NASB).

Fear causes us to withdraw and hide. Fear is a type of self-preservation. Strong fear becomes dread. A violent or paralyzing fear is called terror. A combination of fear, aversion, and repugnance is termed "horror." If fears are persistent and doubts increase, worry is born. If worry turns to apprehension or uneasiness, it becomes anxiety.

The moods of fear and worry are characterized by a combination of the following feelings:

Overwhelmed	Alone
Anguished	Sad
Timid and shy	Scared
Miserable	Frantic
Discouraged	Nervous
Weighed down	Troubled

The moods of fear and worry also create physical responses. These symptoms include: excessive perspiration, muscle tension, headaches, abdominal pain, ulcers, and nausea. With enough thoughts of fear you can experience diarrhea, high blood pressure, rapid heartbeat, fainting, impotence, and frigidity. Often people who are filled with worries and fears sigh a lot, hyperventilate, and have fainting spells. Fear and worry can increase the negative effects of asthma, arthritis, loss of sleep, neck pain, and back pain. People can even experience temporary paralysis and loss of weight due to fear and worry.

The emotion of fear does not generate concern for others, but leads to selfishness. Fear is a feeling of alarm. It is the thought that some danger, pain, or punishment might be impending. We see this in the life of Cain.

And Cain told Abel his brother. And it came about when they were in the field, that Cain rose up against Abel his brother and killed him. Then the LORD said to Cain, "Where is Abel your brother?" And he said,

"I do not know. Am I my brother's keeper?" And He said, "What have you done? The voice of your brother's blood is crying to Me from the ground. And now you are cursed from the ground, which has opened its mouth to receive your brother's blood from your hand. When you cultivate the ground, it shall no longer yield its strength to you; you shall be a vagrant and a wanderer on the earth." And Cain said to the LORD, "My punishment is too great to bear! Behold, Thou hast driven me this day from the face of the ground; and from Thy face I shall be hidden, and I shall be a vagrant and a wanderer on the earth, and it will come about that whoever finds me will kill me" (Genesis 4:8-14 NASB).

Cain's guilt and fear became his central focus. Although he killed his brother without remorse, he became fearful that someone would kill him. His thinking turned inward and became self-centered. This is evident when Cain says "I" and "me" six different times:

"*My* punishment"
"Thou has driven *me*"
"*I* shall be hidden"
"*I* shall be a vagrant"
"Whoever finds *me*"
"Will kill *me*"

One of the best ways to kill the giants of fear and worry is to take your eyes off yourself and begin to think of others. If you were to look at the amount of time you spend thinking about a particular problem, would the greater portion be about you and your well-being, or about other people? It is easy to make ourselves the center of attention—if not in everyone else's mind, at least in our own. The "poor-me syndrome" is a natural offshoot of inward thinking.

The healthiest people are those who have given themselves to helping others. Paul the apostle encourages us to do this in 1 Corinthians 10:24 (NASB): "Let no one seek his own good, but that of his neighbor."

"But that is not easy," you say.

Of course not. Who said it would be easy? The path of least resistance is to moan and groan and feel sorry for ourselves. The difficult but rewarding path is to deny ourselves the luxury of self-pity. Television talk shows are filled with people who whine about their lives. They grumble about relationships. They snivel and whimper that they are victims. It is time to face our fears and hurts head-on. They won't go away unless we confront them.

One ought never to turn one's back on a threatened danger and try to run away from it. If you do that, you will double the danger. But if you meet it promptly and without flinching, you will reduce the danger by half. Never run away from anything. Never!
—*Winston Churchill*

So the LORD said to him, "Therefore whoever kills Cain, vengeance will be taken on him sevenfold." And the LORD appointed a sign for Cain, lest anyone finding him should slay him (Genesis 4:15 NASB).

The Bible does not say what type of mark or sign was put on Cain. Some scholars think it was some kind of tattoo. I think it was an attitude and a lifestyle. Cain's life became a sign or example of what not to do. He passed on to his children a legacy of dysfunction. This dysfunction is seen in Genesis 4:23,24 (NASB):

> And Lamech said to his wives, "Adah and Zillah, listen to my voice, you wives of Lamech, give heed to my speech, for I have killed a man for wounding me; and a boy for striking me; if Cain is avenged sevenfold, then Lamech seventy-sevenfold."

At the fifth generation, Lamech is born to the line of Cain. Lamech becomes the first bigamist in the Bible. He also has Cain's temper. He murders a man and a boy for crossing him. He lets his wives know their place and warns them of their possible fate. Cain's legacy is passed down to his ancestry. After the murder of Abel, Seth was born to Adam and Eve. It is from the line of Seth that Christ was born.

Is ancestry important? Take a look at the descendants of two men who lived in early America: one a devout Christian minister; the other an outspoken unbeliever:

> The minister was Jonathan Edwards. He married a devout Christian girl. From their union have come 729 descendants. They include 300 ministers, 65 college professors, 13 university presidents, 60 authors of good books, 3 U.S. congressmen, and 1 vice-president of the United States. The only known black sheep was Aaron Burr, grandson of

Edwards, a brilliant politician who turned away from his family's faith.

The unbeliever was Max Jukes who lived not far from the Edwards. He married an unbeliever and they produced 1,026 known descendants, 300 died early in life. One hundred went to prison for an average of thirteen years each. Twice that number were public prostitutes. Another 100 were drunkards. The family cost the state over one million dollars. They made little contribution to society.[1]

If you read the story of Cain carefully, you will note that he never confessed his sin. Nor did he ask for repentance. He only complained and wallowed in self-pity that his punishment was too great to bear. How typical that is of our society today. There is far more energy spent on defending the rights of the perpetrators of crime than on protecting the rights of the victims.

Cain then left the presence of the Lord. You will notice in Genesis 4:16 that God did not leave Cain, but he left God. He went to the land of Nod. The name "Nod" means "wandering." When you leave the presence of the Lord, you begin to wander. You experience loneliness, fear, and worry. There is no joy, fruit, or peace to those who run from God.

Is There Such a Thing as Good Fear?

God created our emotions, and they help to give us richness and fullness. Our emotions alert us to what is important in life. Our emotions can be our best friends or our worst enemies.

Fear is a healthy emotion when it keeps us from getting too close to the edge and falling from a high place. Fear helps us to protect our young children as they wander into the street. Fear causes us to drive safely on a busy freeway. The emotion of fear can be a protection device to save us from emotional or physical harm.

Fear is beneficial when we begin to fear God. King Solomon talked about this when he said, "The fear of the LORD is the beginning of knowledge" (Proverbs 1:7 NASB). Solomon went on to instruct us that the fear of God is good for our physical health: "The fear of the LORD prolongs life, but the years of the wicked will be shortened" (Proverbs 10:27 NASB).

Matthew informs us that of all the fears in life, the most important one is the one that reminds you of your eternal destiny: "And do not fear those who kill the body, but are unable to kill the soul; but rather fear Him who is able to destroy both soul and body in hell" (Matthew 10:28 NASB).

Fear That Destroys

If you are not careful, you can be overwhelmed by fears. Newspapers and television alert our fears of gang violence and drive-by shootings. Some people are afraid to drive down the street because of drunk drivers on the road. Others are concerned that they may be robbed or assaulted as they go to the store. Many are hesitant to eat in fast-food restaurants because of stories of food poisoning.

I can remember walking to school as a young child and being afraid that I would hurt my mother. Some older child told me that if I would step on a crack (in the sidewalk) that I would break my mother's back.

Fear has run rampant in our society. Fears have paralyzed many people and have increased so much that we now categorize various fears as phobias. I have read of over 200 different fears that are now classified as phobias. It has gotten to the point that it is simply ridiculous.

Fear of People

* Androphobia (men)
* Agoraphobia (crowds)
* Theophobia (God)
* Gynephobia (women)
* Harpaxophobia (robbers)
* Satanophobia (Satan)

Fear of Animals

* Musophobia (mice)
* Ornithophobia (birds)
* Arachnephobia (spiders)
* Herpetophobia (reptiles)
* Vermiphobia (worms)
* Pediculophobia (lice)

Fear of Things

* Belonephobia (needles)
* Hydrophobia (water)
* Pogonophobia (beards)
* Mysophobia (dirt)
* Phonophobia (telephones)
* Petronophobia (feathers)

Fear of Natural Phenomena

* Astrapophobia (lightning)
* Pyrophobia (fire)
* Drosiphobia (body odor)
* Aerophobia (draft)
* Sciophobia (shadows)
* Cryophobia (frost)

Fear of Situations

* Hygrophobia (dampness)
* Chromophobia (color)
* Ideophobia (ideas)
* Eleutherophobia (freedom)
* Tachophobia (speed)
* Rhabdophobia (magic)

Fear of Places

* Hypsophobia (high places) * Claustrophobia (tight places)
* Limnophobia (lakes) * Thalassophobia (sea)
* Ecclesiophobia (church) * Uranophobia (heaven)

Fear of Activities

* Graphophobia (writing) * Phagophobia (swallowing)
* Stasophobia (standing) * Katagelophobia (ridicule)
* Cliophobia (going to bed) * Gephyrophobia (crossing bridges)

I think it would save a lot of time and energy if everyone would simply adopt "Panphobia." Panphobia is the fear of everything.

Fear and Worry Are Futile

How much time have you spent worrying about a particular problem? How much energy has been drained from you by fear? What is the result of the use of all this time and energy? Has it changed anything?

I have a friend who tells me that it pays to worry about things. He says that 99 percent of the things he worries about never happen. He says worry helps to keep them away.

God has different thoughts about worry and anxiety. He suggests that anxiety cannot change a thing in our lives.

> For this reason I say to you, do not be anxious for your life, as to what you shall eat, or what you shall drink; nor for your body, as to what you shall put on. Is not life

more than food, and the body than clothing? Look at the birds of the air, that they do not sow, neither do they reap, nor gather into barns, and yet your heavenly Father feeds them. Are you not worth much more than they? And which of you by being anxious can add a single cubit to his life's span? And why are you anxious about clothing? Observe how the lilies of the field grow; they do not toil nor do they spin, yet I say to you that even Solomon in all his glory did not clothe himself like one of these. But if God so arrays the grass of the field, which is alive today and tomorrow is thrown into the furnace, will He not much more do so for you, O men of little faith? Do not be anxious then, saying, "What shall we eat?" or "What shall we drink?" or "With what shall we clothe ourselves?" For all these things the Gentiles eagerly seek; for your heavenly Father knows that you need all these things. But seek first His kingdom and His righteousness; and all these things shall be added to you. Therefore do not be anxious for tomorrow; for tomorrow will care for itself. Each day has enough trouble of its own (Matthew 6:25-34 NASB).

Worry is a sin. It is an act of our will where we choose not to trust God. To worry is to say that we know what is better for our lives than God does. It comes from our desire to control everything. When things do not go as we think they should, we become fearful. We worry. We become anxious.

In the previous passage we are told that God cares more for us than for the animals and plants He has created. It is up to us to exercise faith and believe that. God knows what is happening in your life right now. He knows the hurt and pain you feel. He knows how fearful you have been feeling. Can you turn your fears over to Him? Will you turn your fears over to Him?

> Even though I walk through the valley of the shadow of death, I fear no evil; for Thou art with me (Psalm 23:4 NASB).

> The LORD is my light and my salvation; whom shall I fear? The LORD is the defense of my life; whom shall I dread? (Psalm 27:1 NASB).

It is one thing to read the above verses. It is another to believe them. Do you believe that God is with you? If you have received Christ as your Savior, He is with you. Hebrews 13:5 in the Amplified Bible drives home the point that Christ is with us and will not forsake us in all of our troubles:

> For He (God) Himself has said, I will not in any way fail you nor give you up nor leave you without support. [I will] not, [I will] not, [I will] not in any degree leave you helpless, nor forsake nor let [you] down [relax My hold on you].—Assuredly not!

To help diminish the power of fear and worry in your life, you have to confess the sin of your worry. It is the starting point for change. It is admitting to God that you have been attempting to run your life your way. You need to give your life over to God. Give Him your fears. Give Him your concerns. Give Him your worries. That may be very difficult for you because you will have to give up control of your life to Him. Just remember, "God is God, and you are not."

Next, it is important to change your thinking pattern. Rather than thinking about all of the negative things that can happen to you, you need to think about the positive things. You need to have an attitude adjustment. Paul talks about this process in Philippians: "Always be full of joy in the LORD; I say it again, rejoice!" (Philippians 4:4).

He repeats his joy statement twice because we have a tendency not to listen. It is easy to nod our heads and give mental assent without putting it into practice: "Let everyone see that you are unselfish and considerate in all that you do. Remember that the LORD is coming soon" (Philippians 4:5).

As we mentioned earlier, one of the best ways to get rid of worry and fear is to become unselfish and give ourselves to helping others. The Living Bible translates the reason as, "The Lord is coming soon." The New American Standard Bible says, "The Lord is near." I think this is the better translation. We should be unselfish and considerate because "the Lord is near." He is right next to us. He knows what we do. He knows what we think. If we would live our lives as if Christ were physically standing next to us all the time, we would be different people. We would talk differently to others. We would act godly. We would think more positively and less negatively.

> Don't worry about anything; instead, pray about everything; tell God your needs and don't forget to thank him for his answers. If you do this you will experience God's peace, which is far more wonderful

than the human mind can understand. His
peace will keep your thoughts and your
hearts quiet and at rest as you trust in Christ
Jesus (Philippians 4:6,7).

Paul reminds us of the importance of prayer. You
will experience God's peace if you change your
thoughts of fear and worry to thoughts of prayer. The
next time you catch yourself worrying about some situation, start praying about that problem. You will be
amazed at what will happen to you.

And now, brothers, as I close this letter
let me say this one more thing: Fix your
thoughts on what is true and good and right.
Think about things that are pure and lovely,
and dwell on the fine, good things in others.
Think about all you can praise God for and
be glad about. Keep putting into practice all
you learned from me and saw me doing,
and the God of peace will be with you
(Philippians 4:8,9).

Have you been frustrated? Has your heart been
filled with fear? Have you been thinking about all of
the good things in others or all of the bad things?
Have you spent most of your time thinking about
pure things? Do you find yourself praising God all
the time? Would you like to experience God's
peace? Then change your thinking process. Start
thinking about good things. This may be difficult
because you have developed such a negative attitude.

Stop right now and put down this book. Ask God to forgive you for your sin of fear and worry. Ask Him to help you to think about all the blessings He has given you.

I am reminded of the story of the man who felt that his life was too difficult. He thought that his problems were overwhelming. He was angry and tired of all the hurt and pain. One day as he was complaining he said, "I wish I could talk to someone in heaven about this mess I'm in."

Poof!

All of a sudden the man found himself in heaven in the presence of St. Peter.

"I understand you don't like the burden you are having to carry," said St. Peter.

"That's right. I think that the cross I have been given to bear is just too heavy."

"Would you like a different one?"

"Yes, I would."

St. Peter took the man into a large room filled with crosses. Some of the crosses were small. Others were enormous. A few of the crosses were rugged and looked very heavy. A couple of them had wheels on them.

"If you don't like the cross you are carrying," said St. Peter, "you can exchange yours for any one in this room."

The man walked around the room looking at various crosses. Many of them were taller than he was. Eventually, he found a very tiny cross stuffed back in the corner behind a very weather-beaten and rugged cross. It was smooth and polished and could fit in the palm of his hand.

"I would like this one," said the man.

"Good choice," said St. Peter. "That's the one you've been carrying."

The Most Difficult Word in the English Language

As human beings, we will do almost anything to avoid pain and suffering. We will drink alcohol to dull our painful emotions. We will swallow pounds of pills to avoid the discomfort of loss. We will yell and scream about our problems. We will pretend that they don't exist. We will try to escape from difficulties through "going crazy" or suicide. Christ Zois in his book *Think Like a Shrink* suggests that the hardest word in the English language is the word *good-bye*:

> The ability to say good-bye is one of the cornerstones of mental health. Your ongoing ability to tolerate losses of all kinds—death, divorce, altered circumstances, a change of jobs, retirement, a loss of money, estrangement from someone close to you—is determined by your past experiences of loss, including those that occurred in your earliest years, as well as the way you deal with your strong emotions—anger, hurt, and guilt. The most constant experience in life is change, and we very often equate change with loss.

Much worry and fear has to do with loss—the actual loss of something or the possibility of loss. This can be a loss of self-esteem, of relationships, of finances, or of health.

Since we cannot determine the future, we need to learn to relax and give the future to God. He cares for us more than for the sparrows of the field and the lilies of the valley.

All the Days of My Life

The Lord is my shepherd—
    All the days of my life
I shall not want—
    All the days of my life
He maketh me to lie down in green pastures—
    All the days of my life
He leadeth me beside the still waters—
    All the days of my life
He restoreth my soul—
    All the days of my life
He leadeth me in the paths of righteousness
for his name's sake—
    All the days of my life
Yea, though I walk through the valley of the
shadow of death—
    All the days of my life
I will fear no evil—
    All the days of my life
For thou art with me—
    All the days of my life
Thy rod and thy staff they comfort me—
    All the days of my life
Thou preparest a table before me in the
presence of mine enemies—
    All the days of my life
Thou anointest my head with oil—
    All the days of my life
My cup runneth over—
    All the days of my life
Surely goodness and mercy shall follow me—
    All the days of my life
And I will dwell in the house of the Lord forever—
    All the days of my life.

                                        —Psalm 23

Dear God,

I sure spend a lot of time thinking about things I cannot change. I am tired of losing sleep and dealing with stress and tension. I want to be done with all the headaches.

I hate to admit it but my focus has been very selfish and self-centered. Please help me to get my mind off my troubles and problems. Help me to think of others. Please give me the ability to meet their needs when they go through deep waters.

Help me to change my thinking process. It is so easy to think about the negative rather than the positive. Help me to look for the good in people and situations.

Help me to realize that you will never leave me nor forsake me. Help me to know that you are by my side. Help me to love people as you would love them.

Attitude Check

Please read the following questions and rate your present attitude on a scale of 1 to 10. If you circle a 1, you would be saying that your attitude is low or negative. If you circle a 10, you would be saying your attitude is high or very positive. Rate your honest feelings at this time in your life.

		Negative (Low)							Positive (High)		
1.	My employer would rate my job performance and attitude as a	1	2	3	4	5	6	7	8	9	10
2.	The fellow workers at my job or my school friends would rate me with an attitude of	1	2	3	4	5	6	7	8	9	10

		Negative (Low)							Positive (High)		

3. My family, who really know me, would say that my attitude at home would deserve a   1 2 3 4 5 6 7 8 9 10

4. The way I respond to or get along with friends and strangers would give me a rating of   1 2 3 4 5 6 7 8 9 10

5. The way I deal with daily frustrations, along with my patience and tolerance level would give me a number   1 2 3 4 5 6 7 8 9 10

6. The amount of care, concern, and sensitivity that I show to others would give me a rating of   1 2 3 4 5 6 7 8 9 10

7. My happiness level and the sense of humor I display would give me a number   1 2 3 4 5 6 7 8 9 10

8. My enthusiasm toward life and my work at this period would register the rating of   1 2 3 4 5 6 7 8 9 10

9. My overall view of my attitude at this time would get a realistic rating of   1 2 3 4 5 6 7 8 9 10

10. If God were to rate my present attitude, I think He would give me a number   1 2 3 4 5 6 7 8 9 10

A score of 90 or above	Great attitude—pass it on.
A score of 70 to 90	A few minor adjustments suggested.
A score of 50 to 70	Major adjustments are recommended.
A score of 50 or below	Time for a complete overhaul.[2]

When a man is gloomy, everything seems to go wrong; when he is cheerful, everything seems right! (Proverbs 15:15).

1. Make a list of the things you have been worrying about: _____
   _____
   _____
   _____
   _____
   _____
   _____
   _____

2. Turn the above list into a prayer list. Turn these worries over to God.

3. Make a list of people whom you can help. This will help you to turn from an inward focus to an outward focus. As you list their names, write down how you think you might help them.

   _____
   _____
   _____
   _____
   _____

4. Make a list of attitudes that you would like to see God change during the next month. Be specific. _____

_____

_____

_____

_____

_____

_____

_____

_____

_____

Verses to Look Up

Psalm 34:4
Psalm 37:25
Proverbs 1:33
Proverbs 10:27

Isaiah 41:10
Isaiah 43:1,2
Jeremiah 1:8
Romans 8:15,16

CHAPTER THIRTEEN

How to Handle Stress

He who rides a tiger is afraid to dismount.

—*Chinese proverb*

Our heads jerked when we heard the screech of brakes. We looked up just in time to see an incredible scene. The driver of the noisy car threw open his door and jumped out while the car was still moving. He tossed himself on the street in front of an oncoming truck.

There was another screech of brakes. The quick-thinking truck driver somehow got his truck stopped, just inches before running over the man who had leaped from the car.

The man who had jumped from the car got to his feet and began to run down the alley by our office. A woman who had been riding in the car slid over into the driver's seat of the rolling vehicle. She began to pursue the man who was running down the alley.

We ran out of the office and tried to get the license number of the car. By the time we got to the alley, they were too far away to see the license plate. We had just witnessed an attempted suicide.

It takes a great deal of stress in a person's life to bring him to the point of suicide. The fast pace of today's society and the complexity of our lifestyles create much tension. The strain of daily living in a rapidly changing world has created much pressure. How did we get to this point?

From the founding of the United States to the mid-1800s, life in America was fairly simple and straightforward. It was a time when the family stayed together for survival. Both parents had definite roles, and the children knew their place and responsibilities.

The name of the game was survival—carving out an existence in the wilderness. Decisions were clear-cut, black-and-white, with very few shades of gray. A man's word was his bond, and hard work was a way of life. Most men followed the same line of work from their youth until they could no longer work.

No, work is not an ethical duty imposed upon us from without by a misguided and outmoded Puritan morality; it is a manifestation of man's deepest desire that the days of his life shall have significance.
—Harold W. Dodds

In the mid-1800s, life began to change. The age of the industrial revolution was born. Families moved out of the country, into the cities. Factories were built. The role of parents began to change. Society began moving from a patriarchal focus to a matriarchal focus. The father gave up much of his child-rearing influence, and the mother began to assume a larger role in education. No longer did the children work with their fathers in the field or in the store.

From the beginning of the industrial revolution to the present time, there have been massive changes in society. Family roles have changed, and the destruction of the traditional family unit has increased. Divorce and unwed motherhood are common. Overcrowding and the noise level found in cities have almost become accepted as a way of life. Ethnic disputes and political infighting are everyday occurrences. Crime and drug abuse abound.

Economic pressures, layoffs, and job stress are issues that affect most families. Today, a man changes his vocation an average five to seven times during his life. This change of lifestyle, coupled with a society that is constantly on the move, has created much stress and disruption in the lives of millions of people.

The name of the game is still survival, but the rules and complexity of life have changed dramatically. The changes are almost overwhelming. The light at the end of the tunnel may be a train coming toward us.

It seems as if someone has pushed the fast-forward button on life.

"I want the merry-go-round to stop! I can't take it anymore! Just when I start to get ahead, someone gets sick in the family. Last week a crazy driver ran into my car. He didn't have any insurance. And on top of all that, my boss just told me that in the next layoff I am the low man on the totem pole. Will it ever end?" said Art as he collapsed into a chair in my office.

"I can't keep up with the pressure. My daily schedule is so full that I think I'm going to explode." Karen began to cry as she shared her story. Karen was a working mother with three children. "I don't have any energy left. After I make breakfast, fix the lunches, go to work, pick the kids up after soccer practice, make dinner, wash the dishes, and put in a load of clothes, I can hardly stand up. My husband Jim works all day and then goes to night school. He is trying to learn some computer skills so that he can get a promotion. We hardly see each other anymore. There must be more to life than this."

One of the curses that faced Cain in Genesis 4 was that the ground would no longer yield its strength to him. God said a similar thing to Adam and Eve in Genesis 3:17-19 (NASB).

> Cursed is the ground because of you; in toil you shall eat of it all the days of your life. Both thorns and thistles it shall grow for you; and you shall eat the plants of the field; by the sweat of your face you shall eat bread, till you return to the ground, because from it you were taken; for you are dust, and to dust you shall return.

Just as Adam and Eve and Cain were faced with hard work, so are we. It is the common lot of mankind. However, man sometimes adds to God's curse by piling on work pressures.

"Stress" and "burnout" are common terms today. Doctors, counselors, and ministers are overwhelmed with the load of helping people cope with this fast-paced society. Time pressures are overpowering. The desire to keep up with trends and the thirst for material goods pushes everyone to the breaking point.

The constant pressure to be something more than we are or to do something more creates unrealistic goals. Because of poor coping skills or poor time management, many people develop the "workaholic" mind-set. The overabundance of activity and unspoken expectations causes many individuals to neglect their own health.

Every good and excellent thing stands moment by moment on the razor's edge of danger and must be fought for.

George was a good example of this. He was the vice president of a small corporation. He was so busy that often he would skip meals to get his work done. What he did not get done between 8 A.M. and 5 P.M., he stuffed into his briefcase to take home with him.

George lived his life on high-sugar foods and gallons of coffee. He did not have time to exercise or relax in any form. He did not allow himself a minute to just sit and think or plan. George began to take Valium to help him cope. He took Tagamet for stomach ulcers, and Inderal for his high blood pressure, angina, and migraine headaches.

Everyone who looked at George thought he was a very successful businessman. He was, until he had his first heart attack. Now in the hospital, he is evaluating just how successful he really was.

The human body cannot withstand stress and pressure for an extended period of time without some form of negative response. The negative responses are like little red flags that wave in the wind. They are waving, trying to get our attention. Too often we ignore the waving of the body's flags. They are trying to tell us that we are under too much stress. We have overridden our body's cry for help and relief so often that we do not even recognize our stress indicators. Following is the Stress Alert Indicator. It is designed to help remind you of the many different ways your body tries to protect itself from further damage. Have you been listening to your body lately? Do you need to slow down a little?

I am reminded of the story of the little boy who wanted to play ball with his father, but his father was working late.

Little Jeff:	Mom, how come Daddy is never home? He never comes to my games. Doesn't he want to do anything with me?
Mother:	Your father is very busy at work. He has lots to do, and his boss told him that it was a rush job.
Little Jeff:	Couldn't they put Daddy in a slower class?

STRESS ALERT INDICATOR

Stress has a way of building up and leaking out in your body. Check the various signs of stress that may be found in your life at this time. Note the general area where signs are more pronounced. In the future, be aware of this area as a Stress Alert indicator for yourself.

Mood Signs of Stress

❑ Boredom   ❑ Confusion

- ❑ Depression
- ❑ Detachment
- ❑ Disorientation
- ❑ Escape thoughts
- ❑ Feeling low
- ❑ Forgetfulness
- ❑ Impatience
- ❑ Insecurity
- ❑ Irritability
- ❑ Listlessness
- ❑ Nervousness
- ❑ Overexcitement
- ❑ Paranoia
- ❑ Quick-temperedness
- ❑ Sadness
- ❑ Sleep loss
- ❑ Uneasiness
- ❑ Worry

Visceral Signs of Stress

- ❑ Cold chills
- ❑ Cold hands
- ❑ Colitis
- ❑ Cramps
- ❑ Diarrhea
- ❑ Dry mouth
- ❑ Fainting
- ❑ Heartburn
- ❑ Heart pounding
- ❑ Light-headedness
- ❑ Moist hands
- ❑ Nausea
- ❑ Sweating
- ❑ Ulcers

Musculoskeletal Signs of Stress

- ❑ Arthritis
- ❑ Back pain
- ❑ Cramps
- ❑ Fidgeting
- ❑ Fist clenching
- ❑ Grinding teeth
- ❑ Headaches
- ❑ Jaw tightening
- ❑ Shaky hands
- ❑ Stiff neck
- ❑ Stuttering
- ❑ Tense muscles
- ❑ Tics
- ❑ Twitches

Other Signs of Stress

- ❑ Cold sores
- ❑ Compulsiveness
- ❑ Exhaustion
- ❑ Low spiritual life
- ❑ Nail-biting
- ❑ Neglecting family

❑ Fatigue
❑ Frequent colds
❑ Hair-twisting
❑ Hay fever
❑ Heart disease
❑ High alcohol use
❑ High caffeine use
❑ High nicotine use
❑ High sugar use
❑ Jumpiness
❑ Low sex drive
❑ Neglecting friends
❑ Neglecting fun
❑ Neglecting health
❑ Neglecting exercise
❑ Neglecting rest
❑ No enthusiasm
❑ No vigor
❑ Obesity
❑ Obsessiveness
❑ Stained armpits

Stress Is Not Always Bad

There are two sides to stress: the positive side and the negative side. On the positive side, stress helps us perform better and keeps us alive.

If children are left on their own, they will often seek the path of least resistance. Would children eat the right foods without some pressure from parents? Would they do their homework? Would they naturally take music lessons, mow the lawn, and clean their rooms? If a football coach or gymnastics instructor didn't create a little stress in the lives of athletes, would they reach their highest potential?

The drill instructor in a Marine boot camp puts a great deal of stress, strain, and pressure on the new recruits. Why does he do this? It is not for the sheer joy of seeing them suffer (although the recruits may believe this is his reason).

The instructor wants to make his men tough. He wants to build endurance. He wants them to learn to be disciplined and take orders. He knows that there may come a day when the lives of his men will be threatened. The life of each recruit and of the entire group may depend on how they have learned to respond to pressure. Their positive reaction to stress exposure and training will determine their future in staying alive.

On the negative side, too much exposure to stress wears a person out and he ceases to be healthy or productive. It can even lead to death. If stress becomes too intense and the duration is too long, the body's stress indicators come into play. The body may not be able to ward off infections. Small wounds and bruises may not heal as rapidly.

Often you can see the effect of long-term stress in businessmen by looking at their shoulders. Sometimes their right shoulder will be as much as one to two inches lower than their left shoulder. This can be an indicator that they have been weighed down for a period of time. Small children who are under stress may react with bed-wetting. A young person may display acting-out behaviors or may withdraw into silence as a reaction to the strain he is feeling.

The basic reactions to pressure and stress are either fight or flight. The individual may try to resist or do away with the stress, or he may run and escape from it. The response will vary depending on the circumstances. Sometimes it is the best course of action to stand up to the bully who is pushing you around. You may need to teach him that you are not afraid, and that he cannot get his way all the time. On the other hand, when the bully has his entire gang standing behind him and your life may be in the balance, escape may be the proper response. You may save yourself by the quick reaction of turning and running away.

There are three stages to stress: alarm, resistance, and exhaustion. In the alarm stage the body is alerted to the need for action. Adrenaline begins to flow, and the body responds. The next stage is resistance. This is

Stress Cycle

the fight or flight response. However, the body can only fight or flee for so long. It will eventually run out of energy. This leads to the exhaustion stage.

Many individuals have been living next to the exhaustion stage for quite a period of time. They are simply burned out. They need relief and rest. What stage are you at in your experience? Are you feeling good and healthy? Do you feel like taking on the world? Is your energy level high? Are you excited about life? Or are you wanting to get off the merry-go-round of activity? Do you have the desire to escape? Do you want to be left alone for a while? How are you handling stress at this time?

Stress is part of life. Stress can be healthy and fun. This is dramatically seen in such recreational activities as mountain climbing, river rafting, motorcycle riding, and downhill skiing. There can be pleasure from stress-producing events such as stage performances, leadership responsibilities, and public speaking.

The key is not to eliminate stress but to learn to balance it and live with it. We need to learn how to control it where possible. One of the best ways to deal with stress is to have a positive attitude toward life. We can learn to accept the changes of life with an optimistic outlook. We can face the crisis events as opportunities to grow and challenges to gain victory in.

Getting Out of the Frying Pan

Learning how to manage stress or reduce it is important for happiness and survival. It may be time for you to reorganize your priorities. Or you may be someone who has not taken time to even think about goals for healthy living. Now is a good time for reevaluation of your pressures and pace.

> **There are three basic questions in counseling:**
> 1. **What is going on?**
> 2. **How do you feel about it?**
> 3. **Do you want to change?**

I have tried to help you identify what is going on in your body with the Stress Alert Indicators. At the end of this chapter are two more exercises to help you identify areas of concern. They are the Pressure Gauge and the Stress Assessment.

How do you feel about the pressure in your life at this time? Are you feeling in control of your life? Are there some areas of concern? Are you overwhelmed and think that you are at a breaking point because of stress?

Are you hurting enough to change? Have you come to the point where you know that things have to be different? Then the following is for you. I have listed 20 possible ideas and helps for dealing with stress.

1. Are you drinking too much coffee or too many soft drinks? The caffeine in two-and-one-half cups of coffee a day will double the adrenaline in the body. Are you living on an adrenaline high? I had one client who was drinking 20 cups of coffee a day. Along with this, he was drinking numerous cans of pop. We talked about the need to reduce his daily caffeine intake. However, I forgot to mention one thing to him. I forgot to tell him to reduce his intake on a slow basis or he would have withdrawal symptoms. The next time I saw him he told me that he had quit "cold turkey." The result was massive headaches, upset stomach, and the inability to go to work for three days. Use your head and get off the caffeine drug gradually.

2. If you are hooked on sugar, you need to reduce your daily intake of sweets. Try not to eat between meals. Often you will be doing it out of a nervous habit rather than because you are truly hungry and need energy.

3. Drink lots of water and eat high-fiber foods. Your body needs plenty of fluid to flush it out. High-fiber foods are good for the elimination process. Also, reduce the amount of milk you are drinking. You will find a dramatic change in your health, especially if you have allergies.

4. Items such as alcohol, cigarettes, and drugs will not help you eliminate stress. They only help to mask it or make it worse. How serious are you about your health?

5. When was the last time you did consistent exercise? Come on, be honest. Don't give yourself any excuses. Just get out there and do it. There are books on walking, running, and biking. There are clubs or gyms in your area. When you exercise properly, your body will release endorphins. They help to relax the body. They are also a natural appetite suppressant. That is why it is important for weight reduction to combine healthy eating with exercise.

6. Practice stretching exercises. When under stress, the muscles of the body have a tendency to contract and tighten up. This causes back and neck pain, and headaches. Exercises of bending over and touching your toes will stretch back and leg muscles. When you are in the office, you can sit back as far as possible in a chair and do two exercises. The first is to bend forward in between your knees and stretch your back. The second is to sit with your shoulders and back straight and drop your head forward and slowly rotate it. This will loosen the neck muscles that help to create tension headaches.

7. To help reduce headaches, massage the muscles around the eyes. This is done by making circular massaging strokes with your hands. Do this about every 45 minutes during the day. Concentrate on massaging the area right between your eyes and at the top of the bridge of your nose.

8. You may want to relax by taking what is called a "power nap." A power nap is done by slowly counting to 20 with your eyes closed, while you are in a comfortable chair. As you slowly count, think about relaxing on a warm, sandy beach by the ocean or in a grass field in

the mountains. Visualize the scene in your mind. When you get to 20, slowly count backward to 1, all the time enjoying the quiet spot in your mind.

9. You can also relax by the use of "power breathing." Slowly inhale to the count of ten in your mind. Hold your breath for a slow count of ten. Then slowly let your breath out for the count of ten. Repeat this exercise . . . you guessed it . . . ten times.

10. If you are stressed out when you arrive home, try lying on the floor with your legs up on a chair. This will help to relax your back muscles and get some blood circulation to your head. Pull a pillow under your neck to to fill the hollow space between the back of your head and shoulders. Grab the outside edges of the pillow and bring them toward your chin. This will keep your head from moving to either side and will allow your neck muscles to relax.

11. Make a decision to not take your work home.

12. Try and not take any phone calls between 9 A.M. and 11 A.M. This is a highly productive time for many people. Take and make your phone calls between 11 and 12.

13. Try and reduce your habit of doing two things at the same time (talking on the phone and writing at the same time, planning while you are in the shower, or reading while you are eating). Relax a little. Smell the roses.

14. When faced with a pressure, ask yourself, "Will this matter one year from now or five years from now?

Will it matter in the light of eternity? Is it really that important?"

15. Don't overschedule yourself. Look over your calendar for this next year. Are there any things you should cut out? Do you need to get off some committee? Do you need to delegate a job to someone else? Are you helping others to grow by giving them responsibilities? Or, are you caught up in the false idea that only you can do the job right? To keep a proper perspective about your importance, stick your hand in a bucket of water. Now pull it out. Look at the impression you left behind. You won't die if you let go of some unnecessary responsibilities.

16. What do you need to say no to? Why are you afraid to say no? Do you say yes so people will need you? Do you say yes because you want all the glory? Do you say yes because you want people to like you? You will feel better when you learn to say no. You will find that the world will not collapse if you say no. When you say no, people will try to get you to change your mind. Just keep this thought in mind: *What part of the word no do you not understand?*

17. Take time for some hobbies, listening to your favorite music, or visiting a museum.

18. Take time for your family. Imagine that your family is a very important customer or client. How would you treat that customer? Would you be surly and impatient with him? Would you ignore or yell at him? Then don't do it with your family. For the first 30 minutes when you come home, give your undivided attention to your family members. Treat them as very special,

even if you have had a very busy and pressure-filled day. You will be amazed at how your own stress level will diminish as you give yourself to others.

19. Experiment with letting someone else go first or get in line ahead of you. This may be a new experience for you. Allow someone to cut you off on the highway. Don't yell at or chase after the person, trying to right all the wrongs in the world. Smile and laugh at the ridiculous thought of how silly it is to get worked up over such an unimportant issue. Keep a record of the number of times you allow someone to get ahead without you getting mad or even. It may surprise you.

20. Jesus said, "I have come that they may have life, and have it to the full" (John 10:10 NIV). Are you experiencing a full life? He also said, "I am come that you may have peace." Are you encountering peace? Maybe some of the stress is getting to you because you have not been spending time developing your spiritual life. When was the last time you spent a significant amount of time in prayer or Bible study? Do you suppose it might be possible that if you spent time with God that your attitude and viewpoint on life would change dramatically? There is one way to find out, isn't there?

Dear God,

I feel like I am at the point of exhaustion. I just don't have the time or energy to get all the things done that are pressing on me. My daily schedule tires me just to think about it.

I am worn out from family obligations and job responsibilities. The financial pressures that I am under are overwhelming. My candle has been burning at both ends. I don't see any relief.

I'm tired of being grouchy and angry. I am tired of tension headaches and an upset stomach. I am tired of all the neck and back pain.

Please help me to get organized. Please help me to learn how to say no. Help me to set aside time to get alone with You. Help me to see life from Your viewpoint. Help me to do the important things in life rather than the urgent things.

Pressure Gauge

Below are listed events which occur in the process of living. Place the number of points in the empty right-hand column for each of those events that have happened to you during the *last 12 months.* This is the famous Holmes & Rahe Stress Test.

Life Event	Point Values	
Death of spouse	100	_____
Divorce	73	_____
Marital separation	65	_____
Jail term	63	_____
Death of a close family member	63	_____
Personal injury or illness	53	_____
Marriage	50	_____
Fired from work	47	_____
Marital reconciliation	45	_____
Retirement	45	_____
Change in family member's health	44	_____
Pregnancy	40	_____
Sex difficulties	39	_____
Addition to family	39	_____
Business readjustment	38	_____
Change in financial status	38	_____
Death of close friend	37	_____
Change to different line of work	36	_____

Change in number of marital arguments . . . . 35 _____
Mortgage or loan over $10,000 . . . . 31 _____
Foreclosure of mortgage or loan . . . . 30 _____
Change in work responsibilities . . . . 29 _____
Son or daughter leaving home . . . . 29 _____
Trouble with in-laws . . . . 29 _____
Outstanding personal achievement . . . . 28 _____
Spouse begins or stops work . . . . 26 _____
Starting or finishing school . . . . 26 _____
Change in living conditions . . . . 25 _____
Revision of personal habits . . . . 24 _____
Trouble with boss . . . . 23 _____
Change in work hours, conditions . . . . 20 _____
Change in residence . . . . 20 _____
Change in schools . . . . 20 _____
Change in recreational habits . . . . 19 _____
Change in church activities . . . . 19 _____
Change in social activities . . . . 18 _____
Mortgage or loan under $10,000 . . . . 17 _____
Change in sleeping habits . . . . 16 _____
Change in number of family gatherings . . . . 15 _____
Change in eating habits . . . . 15 _____
Vacation . . . . 13 _____
Christmas season . . . . 12 _____
Minor violations of the law . . . . 11 _____

Total Pressure Point Score . . . . _____

Scores of 0 to 149

Indicate a healthy state with normal stress.

Scores of 150 to 300

Indicate that you will be 50 percent likely to encounter illness within the next six months. Your stress and pressure level decreases your body's ability to ward off illness.

Scores of 301 or more

Indicate that you will be 80 percent likely to encounter illness within the next six months. You need to guard your physical well being by getting sufficient rest, exercise, and proper nutrition. You would be very wise to decrease major changes in your life at this time. Be careful about making career changes, financial investments, or further damaging any relationships. You do not need any more stress, pressure, or change in your life. It is important that you regroup your thoughts and seek counsel for decisions. Try and eliminate as many stress areas as possible.

And the peace of God, which passes all understanding, will keep your hearts and minds through Christ Jesus (Philippians 4:7).

Stress Assessment

	Almost Always True	Often True	Seldom True	Almost Never True
1. I get upset with slow drivers in front of me. I try to get around them.	4	3	2	1
2. I don't like big crowds. I try to avoid them whenever possible.	4	3	2	1
3. I dislike standing in long lines.	4	3	2	1
4. I like to have a lot of room (space) to live and work in.	4	3	2	1
5. I get irritated inside when I am busy at some task and get disturbed.	4	3	2	1
6. I often do not have enough time to get all my work done.	4	3	2	1
7. If too many things happen at one time, I tend to become confused.	4	3	2	1
8. Often I wish that I had help to get everything done.	4	3	2	1
9. I think that people expect too much from me and I feel overwhelmed with demands.	4	3	2	1

		Almost Always True	Often True	Seldom True	Almost Never True
10.	I get depressed when I think of all the tasks that need my attention.	4	3	2	1
11.	I often skip a meal so that I can get some work completed.	4	3	2	1
12.	Many times I get the feeling that I have too much responsibility.	4	3	2	1
13.	I don't like repetitive tasks. I like to work on something different every time.	4	3	2	1
14.	I find that I relax best by keeping busy.	4	3	2	1
15.	I hate to be alone. I seek to belong to some social group.	4	3	2	1
16.	I like to be in control of my life. I don't like someone else making my decisions.	4	3	2	1
17.	I tend to let it depress me more than I should when I don't succeed at things.	4	3	2	1
18.	I often "race against the clock" to save time.	4	3	2	1

	Almost Always True	Often True	Seldom True	Almost Never True
19. I tend to lose my temper when I find that I am under a lot of pressure.	4	3	2	1
20. I tend to do two things at once, like eating at work, and planning while driving or bathing.	4	3	2	1
21. I tend to relive a crisis over and over even though it has passed.	4	3	2	1
22. I tend to worry and I have a difficult time sleeping at night.	4	3	2	1
23. I find that my face becomes hot, or my hands become moist and I sweat more than I should.	4	3	2	1
24. My fingers and hands shake, I develop twitches, and I can't sit still.	4	3	2	1
25. I have headaches, a sore neck, back pains, and my muscles become tense or stiff.	4	3	2	1

Total Score _____

0-25 Points   You seem to be handling the stress of life well.

26-40 Points   You should be watching some things.

41-55 Points   Stress is beginning to get to you.

56-70 Points   Red lights are flashing. You need to make changes.

71-99 Points   You are in danger of threatening your physical, mental, emotional, and spiritual well-being.

Discussion Section

1. Of the various pressures you face, how many have been caused by uncontrolled outside forces? How many have been caused by your not being organized?

2. Do you have added pressures or responsibilities because you were unable to say no? What should be done to change this?

3. What changes would you like to see in your life with regard to emotional health, physical health, and spiritual health?

4. What would be five possible ways to eliminate stress in your life? What tasks should be completed? What tasks should be ignored?

5. Is it better to start with solving the hardest problem facing you, and then everything would be down hill from there? Or, is it better to start with the smallest problem facing you, and develop energy and motivation to take on the harder problems?

Verses to Look Up

Proverbs 16:3	Ephesians 3:16
Isaiah 26:3	Philippians 4:6
John 14:27	1 Thessalonians 5:24
John 16:33	1 Peter 5:7

CHAPTER FOURTEEN

Praising God in the Midst of Problems

> *Difficulty, my brethren, is the nurse of great-*
> *ness—a harsh nurse, who roughly rocks her*
> *foster-children into strength and athletic proportion.*

I have what I call my "back-to-nature philosophy." I guess it is just one way to look at problems. It is a way to learn how to accept hurt and make peace with pain. Let me illustrate by way of a story.

Imagine that it was the 1880s and you and your family had headed west in a covered wagon. Your desire was to get to California and purchase some land. You wanted to start a new way of life.

When you arrived at the base of the Rocky Mountains, you realized that it was too late in the season to cross the passes. They would all be snowed in. You and your family decide to winter in a valley. You and your husband spend many hard hours building a log and sod house to provide winter protection. The children help the best they can for their ages.

One day your husband says, "Honey, you've been working hard for such a long time. Why don't you take the day off and go into town? I'll watch the kids."

Your heart jumps for joy and excitement. You go and change clothes and harness the horses to the wagon, and then drive into town. It is about a five-mile journey, and you enjoy the countryside on the way.

As you drive into town, there is lots of noise. It is filled with people scurrying around tending to their business. You pull up in front of the newspaper office and tie off the horses. As you turn around you see the dress shop. You walk over the dusty street, step up on the boardwalk, and look at the latest fashions displayed. You go in and buy some gingham to make a dress for your daughter and some flannel for shirts for your husband and son. You even buy some fancy ribbon for yourself.

It is a happy and carefree day as you purchase some sugar, flour, salt, and other supplies in the local store. You even treat yourself to lunch at the new restaurant in town.

On the way back home, you find yourself singing and looking at the beautiful snowcapped mountains. As you near home, you see some smoke in the sky. It brings a warm feeling as you think about your fireplace, family, and home.

And then it happens. Your heart and breathing almost stop. You pull up the horses and look in the direction of home. There is too much smoke. Your heart sticks in your throat, and you hit the horses with the whip. You are hardly aware that your store-bought items are bouncing around in the back of the wagon.

As you crest a little rise, you look down and see your cabin in the valley. It is in flames. You can see three bodies on the ground.

Oh, God, no, you say in your mind. You hit the horses and they race toward home. Tears begin to well up in your eyes. As you pull up, you see that your husband and children are on the ground. You leap off the wagon and race to them. It is too late. They are dead. They have been killed during an Indian raid.

What do you do in a case like that? You scream and cry and beat the ground. Your heart breaks in two. You collapse weeping. You cry until there are no more tears left.

Then you get a shovel and dig graves for your family. You wrap their bodies in the new cloth you just purchased. You drag the body of your husband to the grave and place your children beside him. As you begin to throw dirt on their bodies, your crying begins again.

Time passes, and you don't know long you have been on the ground weeping. You finally get up and look around. Your dreams are gone. Your family is gone. You are alone.

What do you do now? You gather a few items that haven't burned and load them in the wagon. You feed and water the horses and fill up the canteens. You get back on the wagon and look around. You only have your memories and a few worldly goods. You tap the horses with the whip and the wagon begins to slowly roll.

You go on with life . . . for that's what it is all about.

Life is not always easy. Along with the joys are many hurts. There are the low times. That's part of living. We have to learn to make peace with what we cannot change and move forward with what we can change.

It is difficulties which show what men are.
—Epictetus

How can I learn to face the tough times? How can

I get on with the business of living? What are the principles for learning how to praise God in the middle of difficulties?

The Bible is a very practical book. Not only does God give us principles for daily living, but He also gives us examples of people who applied His principles to their lives. Perhaps one of the greatest examples of the power of praise is a man named Jehoshaphat. His story is found in 2 Chronicles 20.

The Bible indicates that Jehoshaphat was a righteous man who desired to live for God. Jehoshaphat's life, however, was not free from problems and pressures. He was about 35 years old when a major problem arose in his life.

> It came to pass after this also, that the children of Moab, and the children of Ammon, and with them other beside the Ammonites, came against Jehoshaphat to battle. Then there came some that told Jehoshaphat, saying, There cometh a great multitude against thee from beyond the [Dead] sea on this side Syria; and, behold, they be in Hazazon-tamar, which is Engedi (2 Chronicles 20:1,2 KJV).

To help understand the severity of this problem, we need to know something about the children of Ammon, Moab, and Mount Seir. The children of Ammon were descendants of Lot and were very fierce by nature. They worshiped the god Moloch to whom they offered human sacrifices. They were given to brutish murders, and in one town they thrust out the right eye of all the inhabitants.

The children of Moab were also descendants of Lot. Moab was the grandson of Lot by incest with his eldest daughter. The children of Moab were a constant thorn in the flesh to Israel. When Balak hired Balaam to curse Israel, Balaam instead blessed Israel. Balaam told Balak that the only way he could hinder Israel was not by conquering them but by seducing them. As a result, the Moabite girls entered the camp of Israel and seduced the men. God was angry and sent a plague that destroyed 24,000 men. The children of Moab were very savage and were likened to lions.

The children of Mount Seir were descendants of Esau, the brother who sold his birthright. The inhabitants of the region of Mount Seir were of a very rugged constitution and drove out their enemies before them.

You can imagine what went on in the mind of Jehoshaphat as the various runners raced into this throne room and told him he was being attacked by the "eye jabbers," "the lion men," and the "mountain cutthroats." He had a real problem.

The Last Straw

Do you have problems in your life? You are not alone. Jehoshaphat did not have one problem. He had three problems. That's how it is in life sometimes—one problem brings on another. Like the straw that breaks the camel's back, problems have a way of stacking up until we reach a breaking point in our lives. The secret of joy in your life is how you respond to the problems. How did Jehoshaphat respond?

> And Jehoshaphat feared, and set himself to seek the LORD, and proclaimed a fast throughout all Judah. And Judah gathered themselves together, to ask help of the LORD: even out of all the cities of Judah they came to seek the LORD (2 Chronicles 20:3,4 KJV).

I like Jehoshaphat because he was so human. He was scared to death. His problems put fear into his bones. Have your problems caused you to be a little fearful? Even though Jehoshaphat lived many centuries ago, his life is an example of the proper response to problems and trials.

Jehoshaphat "set himself to seek the LORD" (2 Chronicles 20:3 KJV). This should be our first reaction to the pressures of life. He called a national convention at Jerusalem, proclaimed a fast, and sought the mind of God with regard to his problem.

> Oh God, my God! How I search for you! How I thirst for you in this parched and weary land where there is no water. How I long to find you! How I wish I could go into your sanctuary to see your strength and glory, for your love and kindness are better to me than life itself. How I praise you! I will bless you as long as I live, lifting up my hands to you in prayer. At last I shall be fully satisfied; I will praise you with great joy. I lie awake at night thinking of you—of how much you have helped me—and how I rejoice through the night beneath the protecting shadow of your wings. I follow close behind you, protected by your strong right arm (Psalm 63:1-8).

> I will answer them before they even call to me. While they are still talking to me about their needs, I will go ahead and answer their prayers! (Isaiah 65:24).

> I love the Lord because he hears my prayers and answers them. Because he bends

down and listens, I will pray as long as I breathe! (Psalm 116:1,2).

A Cry for Help

Did you hear about the four men who went mountain climbing? One of the men fell over a cliff, and the other three tried to rescue him. They yelled, "Joe, are you all right?"

"I'm alive, but I think I broke both of my arms."

"We'll toss a rope down to you and pull you up," said the three men.

"Okay," said Joe.

After about a minute, the three men started to pull Joe up. When they had him about three-fourths of the way up, they remembered he had said he had broken both of his arms.

"Joe, if you broke both of your arms, how are you holding on?" they asked.

Joe responded, "With my teeeeeeeeeeth!"

Have you ever felt like you were at the end of your rope just barely holding on with your teeth? Or maybe you have felt so low you had to climb a ladder to touch bottom. This was the case of Jehoshaphat as he called out to God in prayer:

> And Jehoshaphat stood in the congregation of Judah and Jerusalem, in the house of the LORD, before the new court (2 Chronicles 20:5 KJV).

It is wonderful to know we can pray to God anytime and anywhere. God does not require us to be in a particular place or position before He will hear and answer.

I am reminded of the true story of a man who fell down a well. He would have been killed if his legs had not become entangled in the rope that was hanging in the well. It was in this upside-down position that he asked God to come into his life.

What do you think would have happened to the apostle Peter when he was sinking in the water if he would have waited for his evening devotions before crying for help? You can pray with your eyes wide open. When you are driving down the freeway, you can talk to the Lord. The place of prayer is anywhere:

> Art not thou God in heaven? and rulest not thou over all the kingdoms of the heathen? and in thine hand is there not power and might, so that none is able to withstand thee? (2 Chronicles 20:6 KJV).

There is no problem in life too big for God. He is able to meet every situation and circumstance. God is able and willing to meet your need.

> Art not thou our God, who didst drive out the inhabitants of this land before thy people Israel, and gavest it to the seed of Abraham thy friend for ever? And they dwelt therein, and have built thee a sanctuary therein for thy name, saying, If, when evil cometh upon us, as the sword, judgment, or pestilence, or famine, we stand before this house, and in thy presence, (for thy name is in this house), and cry unto thee in our affliction, then thou wilt hear and help (2 Chronicles 20:7-9 KJV).

Because you belong to the family of faith, God is very concerned about your life. He is concerned about every detail. God even has the hairs on your head numbered. Just think of the subtraction problem God has with all the hairs you lose off your head! He can be counted on as being faithful to meet your needs.

> God is our refuge and strength, a tested help in times of trouble. And so we need not fear even if the world blows up, and the mountains crumble into the sea. Let the oceans roar and foam; let the mountains tremble! (Psalm 46:1-3).

> I stand silently before the LORD, waiting for him to rescue me. For salvation comes from him alone. Yes, he alone is my Rock, my rescuer, defense and fortress——why then should I be tense with fear when troubles come? My protection and success come from God alone. He is my refuge, a Rock where no enemy can reach me. O my people, trust him all the time. Pour out your longings before him for he can help! (Psalm 62:5-8).

The Heart of the Problem

> And now, behold, the children of Ammon and Moab and mount Seir, whom thou wouldest not let Israel invade, when they came out of the land of Egypt, but they turned from them, and destroyed them not; behold, I say, how they reward us, to cast us out of thy possession which thou hast given us to inherit (2 Chronicles 20:10,11 KJV).

Many times believers pray "around-the-world prayers." We pray for general things rather than specific needs. It is good to be reminded that God enjoys answering our specific prayers. When we pray that God will work in the lives of everyone in the world, we somehow lose the thrill of seeing answered prayer.

There is a great joy when we pray for specific friends or relatives and they come to know Christ. God wants us to learn to be honest and straightforward in coming to Him with our needs.

> But Jesus the Son of God is our great High Priest who has gone to heaven itself to help us; therefore, let us never stop trusting him. This High Priest of ours understands our weaknesses, since he had the same temptations we do, though he never gave way to them and sinned. So let us come boldly to the very throne of God and stay there to receive his mercy and to find grace to help us in our times of need (Hebrews 4:14-16).

A Cry for Help

> O our God, wilt thou not judge them? For we have no might against this great company that cometh against us; neither know we what to do: but our eyes are upon thee. And all Judah stood before the LORD, with their little ones, their wives, and their children (2 Chronicles 20:12,13 KJV).

Jehoshaphat was a man of prayer and he knew the promises of God. In a time of stress he reached into the memory pack of his mind and drew from the great resources of God.

Jehoshaphat closed his prayer with a very important truth: "We have no might against this great company [problem] that cometh against us. Neither know we what to do: but our eyes are upon thee."

Job said, "Though he slay me, yet will I trust in him" (Job 13:15 KJV). Maybe you have reached this point in your life. Have you come to the end of your resources? Is the difficulty you face overpowering? You are in the perfect position for God to work in your life. Are you ready?

How to Drown

I am reminded of the man and wife who were going through great trials. The husband said, "Well, Martha, we'll just have to trust the Lord!" To which Martha responded, "Has it come to that?"

It seems that many times we have to come to the end of ourselves before we see God begin to resolve our problems. I think He is waiting for us to turn to Him for help.

The story is told of a family who decided to have a family reunion at the beach. Everything was going along fine until the relatives heard a cry for help from the ocean. One of the children had been caught in a small riptide and was being dragged out to sea. None of the relatives was a strong enough swimmer to rescue him.

Not far down the beach they saw a young man and cried for him to assist them. The young man ran down the beach and into the water and stopped when the water reached his knees. He then folded his arms and watched the struggling boy in the water. The relatives urged him to save the boy, but the young man just stood there and ignored them.

After a few minutes the boy in the ocean became very tired and was near sinking under the waves. Instantly the young man dove in the water and swam rapidly to the boy. Before long they were both safe on the beach. The relatives began questioning the young man as to why he waited so long before attempting the rescue.

The young man said, "I am a professional lifeguard. I knew that as long as the boy was struggling in his own strength I would have had a difficult time saving him. He probably would have fought me, and we both might have drowned. I had to wait till he gave up, and then I was able to come to his aid."

God does the same thing with us. He waits until we give up——until we quit trying to solve the problem ourselves. In that moment of time when we give up and quit trying in our own strength, He comes swiftly to our defense and aid.

Within the story of Jehoshaphat we find several principles for dealing with overwhelming problems. If applied, these principles will bring about joy and peace to the child of God.

Principle Number One: The Battle Is Not Yours, but God's

> Then upon Jahaziel the son of Zechariah, the son of Benaiah, the son of Jeiel, the son of Mattaniah, a Levite of the sons of Asaph, came the Spirit of the LORD in the midst of the congregation; and he said, Hearken ye, all Judah, and ye inhabitants of Jerusalem, and thou king Jehoshaphat, Thus saith the LORD unto you, Be not afraid nor dismayed by reason of

this great multitude; for the battle is not yours, but God's (2 Chronicles 20:14,15 KJV).

When a problem crowds into anyone's life, the first two responses are fear and worry. God knows we will react this way. To this reaction He says, "Be not afraid nor dismayed" because of your great problem. "The battle is not yours, but God's."

Is there a problem in your life? It is not yours, it is God's. Let Him take care of it. By faith trust Him for an answer. Do you have a relationship problem with someone? Do you have a troubled marriage? Are your children out of control? Have you encountered financial problems? Are you suffering with health difficulties? Have you given your problem to the Lord?

Do you think that God, who is big enough to run the universe, can handle your difficulty no matter what it is? Of course He can. Then let go. Let God take the burden you have been carrying. Jesus said,

> Come to me and I will give you rest—all of you who work so hard beneath a heavy yoke. Wear my yoke—for it fits perfectly—and let me teach you; for I am gentle and humble, and you shall find rest for your souls; for I give you only light burdens (Matthew 11:28,29).

The battle is not yours but God's.

Principle Number Two:
There Is a Part You Play

> Tomorrow go ye down against them: behold, they come up by the cliff of Ziz; and

> ye shall find them at the end of the brook,
> before the wilderness of Jeruel. Ye shall not
> need to fight in this battle: set yourselves,
> stand ye still, and see the salvation of the
> LORD with you, O Judah and Jerusalem: fear
> not, nor be dismayed; tomorrow go out
> against them: for the LORD will be with you
> (2 Chronicles 20:16,17 KJV).

You may ask, "If the battle is God's, what do I do? Just sit there and twiddle my thumbs?" No, the Bible says that Jehoshaphat had to go out to the battlefield. He had to face the enemy. He had to face his problem.

The Bible is full of stories where the men and women of God had to participate in their difficulties. They exercised their human energy to the fullest and trusted God to do what they could not do. They believed in the God of miracles.

The apostle Paul talks about man's part and God's part when he says, "Work out your own salvation with fear and trembling. For it is God which worketh in you both to will and to do of his good pleasure" (Philippians 2:12,13 KJV). These verses are a good example of two wills involved together.

Restfully Available, Instantly Obedient

To illustrate, let's imagine that one day you woke up to find your right hand running all over your body. And let's say your hand could talk. The conversation might go like this: "What do you think you are doing? You are running all over my body."

"Well," says your hand, "all of us fingers had a meeting and we decided that we are going to do our own thing. We are no longer going to obey you."

What good would a hand like that be? To be of any use and accomplish the wishes of your mind, your hand has to be available to the commands of your mind. When your hand is restfully available and instantly obedient to your mind, your hand literally accomplishes the will of your mind.

God wants you, as a believer, to be restfully available and instantly obedient to His commands. When you are available and obedient, you literally accomplish the will of God in your life.

Let's try an experiment. Please raise this book over your head for a moment and put it down again. If you participated, let me ask, "Whose will raised the book?" You may say, "It was my will. I literally and physically lifted the book." Was the lifting of the book your idea or mine? You may respond, "It must have been your will. It was your idea." Was it? I didn't touch the book. You see, it was a combination of wills. My will was literally and physically fulfilled when you were obedient and lifted the book.

God's will is accomplished in and through your life as you are obedient to the Word of God and the leading of the Holy Spirit.

Principle Number Three:
Thank God for the Victory
Before the Battle Begins

And Jehoshaphat bowed his head with his face to the ground: and all Judah and the inhabitants of Jerusalem fell before the LORD, worshipping the LORD. And the Levites, of the children of the Kohathites, and the children of the Korhites, stood up to praise the LORD God of Israel with a loud voice on high.

> And they rose early in the morning, and
> went forth into the wilderness of Tekoa: and
> as they went forth, Jehoshaphat stood and
> said, Hear me, O Judah, and ye inhabitants
> of Jerusalem; believe in the LORD your God,
> so shall ye be established; believe his
> prophets, so shall ye prosper (2 Chronicles
> 20:18-20 KJV).

It is interesting to note the different ways that the children of Israel praised the Lord. Jehoshaphat and all Judah fell on the ground and praised God. The Kohathites and the Korhites (men of the cloth) stood up and praised God with a loud voice. Both groups were praising God but expressed their praise in a different way. The same is true today. Some express their praise quietly and others with a little more gusto. This does not mean that one group is more spiritual than the other. God allows men and women to express their praise in the context of their own social style. Regardless of the different expressions, both groups were thanking God for the victory before the battle. This is true faith.

The phrase "rose early in the morning" tells us that the children of Israel got a good night's sleep before the battle. They did not stay up all night worrying about the problem. There have been times when I have gone to bed and said, "Father, I don't have any idea how You are going to work out this problem, but I trust You. Thank You in advance for the answer and the victory. I'm tired, and I'll see You in the morning. Thanks again for Your answer. Good night." Does that sound foolish? It's not. It is true faith.

We live by faith or we do not live at all. Either we venture—or we vegetate. If we venture, we do so by faith simply because we cannot know the end of anything at its beginning. We risk marriage on faith or we stay single. We prepare for a profession by faith or we give up before we start. By faith we move mountains of opposition or we are stopped by molehills.
—Harold Walker

In the latter part of verse 20, Jehoshaphat encourages the children of Israel to believe the promises of God. God cannot and will not break a promise. Claim them and rejoice in His fulfillment. When you believe and trust God, you will prosper.

Principle Number Four:
Put the Singers Out in Front

And when he had consulted with the people, he appointed singers unto the LORD, who should praise the beauty of holiness, as they went out before the army, and to say, Praise the LORD; for his mercy endureth forever. And when they began to sing and to praise, the LORD set an ambush against the children of Ammon, Moab, and Mount Seir, who were come against Judah; and they were smitten (2 Chronicles 20:21,22 KJV).

I like the words *consulted* and *appointed*. This tells us that Jehoshaphat talked over his problem and his plan with the people he was leading. It also tells us they were very human. They were scared.

His plan was to send a group of singers (a choir) out in front of the army to say, "Praise the Lord for His mercy endureth forever." How would you like to have been in that singing group as they went into battle before the rest of the army? Can you imagine what the enemy would think as they saw a choir marching toward them? I know the people were afraid because the Bible records that Jehoshaphat "appointed" singers. There were no volunteers.

The word *singers* literally means "praisers." In other words, we need to put the praisers or singers out in front before we go into battle.

There is a key word in verse 22. It is the word *when*. God did not do anything until the praisers began to sing. When they began to sing, God performed a miracle. It is at the point where our faith becomes action that God meets us with a miracle answer. We may not get any volunteers from our emotions at a time of stress. We may have to appoint some singers in our lives by an act of faith and the strength of the will.

God will meet you at the point of faith. Will you join the choir? Will you step out and praise the Lord in the face of your problem?

It is my prayer that God will help you to realize in a new way that the battle is not yours, but God's; that there is a part you play; that you need to thank God for the victory as you put the singers out in front.

Praise—the Will of God

I will praise the Lord no matter what happens. I will constantly speak of his glories and grace. I will boast of all his kindness to me. Let all who are discouraged take heart. Let us praise the LORD together, and exalt his name. For I cried to him and he answered me! He freed me from all my fears (Psalm 34:1-4).

There is an amazing transformation of joy that takes place in the life of the believer who learns to praise God. His whole outlook with regard to problems changes. Those who have not learned to praise God look at the one who does and cannot believe it. They think he is a phony. They wonder how he could really be thankful.

You see, the "praiser" has learned the truth that the flesh does not want to praise God, but his spirit does. He takes that step of faith—even though his emotions cry against it—and praises God. God then meets his faith with a transformation of joy and true peace.

The individual who praises God has learned the truth of 1 Thessalonians 5:18 (KJV), "In every thing give thanks: for this is the will of God in Christ Jesus concerning you." The verse does not say "for every thing give thanks," but "*in* every thing give thanks." Not everything that comes into our lives is good in itself.

No one enjoys the blowout of a tire on the car, the loss of a contact lens, the burn from a hot pan, a fall down the steps, or cancer in the chest. But in the midst of these pressures, there is the experience of joy and peace for the one who will obey the command, "In every thing give thanks."

The "praiser" is also learning the truth of Romans 8:28 (KJV), "And we know that all things work together for good to them that love God." It does not say that all things are good, but that they eventually work together for good.

God's Answer

> And when they began to sing and to praise, the LORD set ambushments against the children of Ammon, Moab, and Mount Seir, which were come against Judah; and they were smitten. For the children of Ammon and Moab stood up against the inhabitants of Mount Seir, utterly to slay and destroy them: and when they had made an end of the inhabitants of Seir, every one helped to destroy another. And when Judah came toward the watch tower in the wilderness, they looked unto the multitude, and, behold, they were dead bodies fallen to the earth, and none escaped (2 Chronicles 20:22-24 KJV).

As Jehoshaphat put the singers out in front, the Lord wiped out the eye jabbers, lion men, and mountain cutthroats. Evidently, each of the attacking armies got greedy and wanted the spoils of Israel and began to fight among themselves. Israel actually went to the battlefield but did not fight the battle. God reminds us that His ways are not our ways.

Treasure Awaits

> And when Jehoshaphat and his people came to take away the spoils of them, they found among them in abundance both riches with the dead bodies, and precious jewels, which they stripped off for themselves, more than they could carry away: and they were three days in gathering of the spoil, it was so much (2 Chronicles 20:25 KJV).

In verse 25, we are told that Israel could not carry away all the spoils of the battle because it was so great. What is the result of praise? It is a "joy unspeakable and full of glory." Paul reminds us that "God shall supply all your need according to his riches in glory by Christ Jesus" (Philippians 4:19 KJV). From the great treasure house of heaven God pours forth His love to us.

Paul goes on to say in Romans 8:37 (KJV), "Nay, in all these things we are more than conquerors through him who loved us." How can one be more than a conqueror? Isn't a conqueror "top dog"? We are more than conquerors by the fact that Christ fought the battle for us and we still receive all of the rewards. May God help us all learn to continually praise Him day by day, moment by moment.

> So the realm of Jehoshaphat was quiet: for his God gave him rest round about (2 Chronicles 20:30 KJV).

Dear God,

I feel like I have been attacked on all sides like Jehoshaphat. My difficulties have been building up for quite a while. I feel like I'm going to be squashed by a big steamroller.

I need Your help. You promised to be there in time of trouble. Well I am in trouble and I would sure appreciate Your appearance—the sooner the better. Give me the strength to hold on and not run in fear.

I am going to grit my teeth and thank You in advance for Your answer to my problem. I don't know how You are going to work it out, but I am going to trust You by faith.

I want to put the singers out in front. I want to thank You for all the great things You have done for me. I certainly don't deserve them. I love You and I trust You. As Job said, "Though he slay me, yet will I trust in him."

CHAPTER FIFTEEN

Looking for a Counselor

Advice is like snow; the softer it falls, the longer it dwells upon, and the deeper it sinks into the mind.

—*Samuel Taylor Coleridge*

Quite a few years ago I remember standing in a phone booth on the grounds of Biola University. I had just gone through a very difficult experience and was feeling quite depressed. I felt all alone and overwhelmed by the emotional pain I was feeling. I needed to talk with someone about the hurt. But it was a Sunday, and the campus was deserted.

I can recall putting money in the coin receiver and dialing the phone number of a friend of mine. I felt certain that he would be able to help lighten the load I was under. The phone rang and I waited. It kept ringing. There was no answer. No one was home.

Have you ever felt like you were all alone with a problem? Have you looked for an answer but no one seemed to be at home?

As the phone was ringing I had an interesting experience. I imagined that I could hear the voice of

God talking with me. Now please do not misunderstand: I do not hear voices. God does not speak audibly to me. He uses the Bible to convey His thoughts. But, nonetheless, I imagined that the conversation went like this:

"Busy number, huh?" asked God.

I imagined that I nodded my head in agreement but did not say a word.

"What are you going to do when you are 25,000 miles away from home on the mission field and you have a problem?"

I could see myself sheepishly looking down at the ground. I still did not reply.

"How are you going to find a phone booth in the middle of a jungle?" God continued to ask. "Who are you going to call at that time?"

I still did not reply. I remember the final questions God asked me in that imaginary conversation.

"When are you going to learn to trust Me? When are you going to learn to call on Me?"

I have never forgotten those words. You see, God is the one Friend who is still there when no one else is around. He is the great Comforter. He is the great Counselor. He gives strength to carry on when we are completely out of energy.

I began to write *What to Do Until the Psychiatrist Comes* because I believe God wants us to learn to trust and walk with Him. He can help us in our times of stress and trouble. We need to learn how to rely on Him for guidance. Sometimes we rely too much on other people.

This does not mean that we should never seek counsel. The Bible encourages us to seek the advice of others. But the Bible also instructs us to learn to have a personal and living relationship with Him.

Through the pages of this book I have endeavored to help you see that everyone on the earth has problems. Difficulties are the common lot of mankind. Just because you have trials does not mean that you are "crazy" or have a "mental illness." It simply means that you are human and you hurt like everyone else. Suffering will be part of your experience as you move from the cradle to the grave. We have seen how people will go to great lengths to avoid pain and suffering.

The truth that many people never understand, until it is too late, is that the more you try to avoid suffering the more you suffer because smaller and more insignificant things begin to torture you in proportion to your fear of being hurt.
—*Thomas Merton*

Out of suffering have emerged the strongest souls; the most massive characters are seared with scars.
—*E. H. Chapin*

I have attempted to help you realize that there is no such thing as mental illness as a disease. There are brain diseases and physical defects that affect the thought and emotional process, but they are not what is commonly referred to as "mental illness."

When we begin to blame some outside source for our problems, we lose the freedom of the human will. It is not these forces that control our happiness; it is our attitude toward the events of life. When we realize this truth, we gain the hope and possibility of change.

It is when we begin to accept responsibility for our

behavior that we begin to mature. This is a painful process because we have to stop shifting blame for our actions to other people. Someone has said, "To err is human. To blame it on the other guy is even more human."

As we grow up, we begin to take ownership of our angers, fears, guilts, and habits. We realize that our emotions can be our friends because they help us to recognize what is important to us. Our emotions and conscience help to expose whether we are living a godly or an ungodly life. As we become aware of our actions, we are confronted with the need to confess our sins. Our sinfulness helps us realize that others need to receive our love and forgiveness. When we forgive them and bury our hurt and anger, we begin to experience God's peace and joy.

The more we begin to praise God, the smaller our problems become. As we focus on the positive things God has done for us, the negative events of life seem to lose their power to destroy us.

On Seeking Counsel from Others

As I mentioned earlier, the Bible has much to say about seeking counsel from other people. Their advice can bring great joy to our lives: "Oil and perfume make the heart glad, so a man's counsel is sweet to his friend" (Proverbs 27:9 NASB).

When we face important decisions in life, it is wise to get different points of view. Good advice will save us from reinventing the wheel and spending needless energy going the wrong direction:

> Where there is no guidance, the people
> fall, but in abundance of counselors there is
> victory (Proverbs 11:14).

Without consultation, plans are frustrated, but with many counselors they succeed (Proverbs 15:22).

Prepare plans by consultation, and make war by wise guidance (Proverbs 24:6).

A wise man is strong, and a man of knowledge increases power. For by wise guidance you will wage war, and in abundance of counselors there is victory (Proverbs 24:5,6).

Many times strange ideas come into our heads. If we think about them long enough, we become confused about whether they are good ideas or bad ideas. Wise counsel will help us to eliminate those ideas that would do us harm.

The way of a fool is right in his own eyes, but a wise man is he who listens to counsel (Proverbs 12:15).

Listen to counsel and accept discipline, that you may be wise the rest of your days. Many are the plans in a man's heart, but the counsel of the LORD, it will stand (Proverbs 19:20,21).

If we have been under emotional stress for a period of time, it is good to have someone help us gain perspective. A different viewpoint is often the very thing that will help us to crystallize the direction we should go: "A plan in the heart of a man is like deep water, but a man of understanding draws it out" (Proverbs 20:5).

Earlier I suggested that there are many questionable practices in the field of psychology. With over 300 different approaches, people have to be careful that they are seeking the mind of God with regard to their problems. Just because an individual has a Ph.D. or M.D. behind his name does not insure that he is a good counselor. I know a number of individuals who have academic degrees behind their names and are less than caring persons. There is little relationship between someone who has credentials and someone who has ability. An official-sounding title does not let you know if the counselor is filled with love, courage, and wisdom. I know many professors who do not have what we call "street smarts." Their personal lives are a disaster.

I am suggesting that you should seek counsel from a godly individual, regardless if he is a professional or a layman. There are many individuals who are just "common folk" and are excellent counselors. They do not make their living from counseling. They just have a godly lifestyle and seek to grow in the knowledge of the Bible.

A good illustration of this is found in a man named Zechariah. He had a job as a combination security guard and policeman. He was a gatekeeper at Solomon's temple. This was how he earned his living.

The Bible does not say much about his job other than he was to protect the north gate. But Zechariah did something else on the side. He had an avocation as a counselor. The Bible says, "Then they cast lots for his son Zechariah, a counselor with insight, and his lot came out to the north" (1 Chronicles 26:14 NASB). Zechariah was not a professional counselor. He was an average man who had much wisdom.

If you feel the need to get additional counsel for the

difficulties you are facing, that is a good idea. The Bible recommends it. When you seek out a counselor, look for someone who has much wisdom.

"How do I find this person?" you ask.

You start by asking God to lead you to the right individual. This person may be a professional counselor, a minister, or a layman. Ask your friends if they know someone like this. Go to your minister. He may be the person, or he could direct you to the right counselor. The news of good counselors often spreads by word of mouth.

When you meet this person, trust your feelings and intuition. Is this someone you like? Do you respect him? Does he have a good reputation? The bottom line is, is he someone you can trust?

He should be an individual who is born again. Someone who has had a personal encounter with Jesus Christ. Someone who will understand and respect your faith.

He should be a person who is spiritually mature and biblically adept. Remember, it is possible to be a "Christian" counselor in name only, and have very little Bible knowledge and not use the Bible in counseling.

He should be someone who is committed to the local church. It is from the church that much growth and nurturing comes. If he is not personally involved in a local fellowship of some kind, I would be most hesitant.

Look for someone who has empathy and the gift of encouragement. A good counselor will instill hope. That is what the "good news" of the Bible is all about. You want someone who is honest and objective. Look for an individual who is a good listener. Rejoice if you find someone who will have courage to lovingly confront you. And look for a counselor who will give you homework assignments and will pray with you.

If he is a professional "Christian" counselor, look for someone who charges reasonable fees. Remember they have to pay the rent and put food on their table also. Someone has said that there are three types of counselors: expensive, costly, and exorbitant. Find someone who is fair.

The most unrewarding task in the world is trying to tell people the truth about themselves before they are ready to hear it; and even Aesop, who cast such truth in fable form, was eventually thrown off a cliff because his morals struck too close to home.
—Sidney Harris

A good counselor will earn his money. It is not an easy task to deal all day with the emotional hurts of others. The counselor understands that change is not usually an overnight event. It is a process, and that process is sometimes painful. One counselor I know calls this process "Forming, Storming, Norming, and Performing."

Forming:	Explaining the details of the problem
Storming:	Going through the pain of growth
Norming:	Getting one's life back to normal
Performing:	Living a healthy life of doing what we should be doing

My prayer is that God will lead you to the place where you begin to experience His peace and joy. I also pray that God will use you to help other people who may be going through similar circumstances.

If finding God's way in the suddenness of storms makes our faith grow broad, then trusting God's wisdom in the "dailyness" of living makes it grow deep. And strong.

Whatever may be your circumstances—however long it may have lasted—wherever you may be today, I bring this reminder: The stronger the winds, the deeper the roots, and the longer the winds . . . the more beautiful the tree.

—Charles R. Swindoll

Counseling Help from the Bible

ABORTION
Jeremiah 1:1-5
Psalm 139:1-24
2 Chronicles 28:1-8

ABUSIVE BEHAVIOR
Romans 12:10
Romans 12:18,19
1 Corinthians 10:31
1 Thessalonians 5:15
James 1:20

ACCOUNTABILITY
Joshua 7:1-15
Judges 6:1-16
Ecclesiastes 12:13,14
Romans 14:1-22

ADULTERY
Isaiah 1:1-31
Hosea 1:1-11
Matthew 5:27-32
Luke 16:16-18
John 8:1-11

ADVICE
Proverbs 1:1-9
Proverbs 6:20-24
Proverbs 10:1-21
Mark 10:17-31

AFFECTIONS
Proverbs 4:23-27

ALCOHOLISM
Proverbs 20:1
Proverbs 23:29-35
1 Corinthians 15:33
2 Peter 2:19

ANGER
Matthew 5:21-26
Ephesians 4:26-32
James 3:6

ANXIETY
Psalm 16:11
Psalm 37:1,7
Proverbs 16:7
Isaiah 41:10

ARGUMENTS
Proverbs 15:1-9
Proverbs 26:17-28
Philippians 2:12-18
Titus 3:1-11

ATTITUDE
Philippians 2:5-11
Philippians 4:4-9

BACKSLIDING

Deuteronomy 8:10-20
Luke 9:57-62
James 5:15-20

BELIEF

Romans 10:5-13
James 2:14-24

BEREAVEMENT

Deuteronomy 31:8
Psalm 23:1-6
Psalm 27:10
Psalm 119:50

BITTERNESS

Hebrews 12:14-17
1 John 3:11-24

CHOICES

Proverbs 1:1-19
Proverbs 13:1-16
Matthew 9:9-13

COMFORT

Job 16:1-22
Lamentations 3:21-26
2 Corinthians 1:3-11

COMPLAINING

Philippians 2:12-18

CONFIDENCE

Matthew 10:26-42
Acts 5:17-26

CONFLICTS

James 4:1-12

CONSCIENCE

Proverbs 28:13-18
Acts 23:1
Acts 24:16
1 Timothy 3:8,9
Hebrews 10:21,22
1 Peter 3:16

CRITICISM

Matthew 7:1-5
Luke 17:1-10
Galatians 5:13-26

DECEIT

Exodus 20:1-21

DEPRESSION

1 Kings 19:1-9
Psalm 42:1-11

DESIRES

Psalm 97:1-12

DESPAIR

Exodus 14:1-14
Psalm 40:1-17

DIFFICULTIES

Romans 8:28
2 Corinthians 4:17
Hebrews 12:7-11
Revelation 3:19

DISAPPOINTMENT

Psalm 43:5
Psalm 55:22
Psalm 126:6
John 14:27
2 Corinthians 4:8-10

DISCOURAGEMENT
Joshua 1:9
Psalm 27:14
Colossians 1:5
1 Peter 1:3-9
1 John 5:14

DISCERNMENT
Matthew 7:1-12
James 1:2-8

DISHONESTY
Proverbs 20:23-30

DISOBEDIENCE
Genesis 3:1-24
1 Chronicles 13:1-14

DIVISIONS
1 Corinthians 4:6-13

DIVORCE and REMARRIAGE
Malachi 2:15,16
Matthew 19:8,9
1 Corinthians 7:10-15

DRINKING
Proverbs 23:29-35
Ephesians 5:15-20

ENCOURAGEMENT
1 Thessalonians 5:1-28
1 Peter 1:1-13

ENTHUSIASM
Colossians 3:18-25

ENVY
Deuteronomy 5:21
1 Kings 21:1-29

ETERNAL LIFE
Luke 18:18-30
John 3:1-21
John 6:60-71
John 17:1-26
1 John 5:1-13

FAULTS
Matthew 7:1-5
Ephesians 4:1-16

FEAR
Joshua 1:1-18
Psalm 27:1
Psalm 56:11
Psalm 91:1-6
Psalm 121:1-8
Proverbs 29:25

FEELINGS
Romans 5:9-21

FOOLISHNESS
Psalm 14:1-7
Proverbs 9:1-18
1 Corinthians 2:6-16

FORGIVENESS
Psalm 51:1-19
Matthew 6:5-15
Matthew 18:21-35
Romans 12:1-21
1 John 1:1-10

FRIENDSHIP
Proverbs 17:1-28
John 15:1-17

FRUSTRATION
Ephesians 6:1-4

GAMBLING
>Proverbs 15:16
>Proverbs 23:4,5
>Luke 12:15
>1 Timothy 6:9

GENTLENESS
>2 Timothy 2:14-26
>James 3:1-18

GOSSIP
>Exodus 23:1-9
>Proverbs 25:18-28
>2 Thessalonians 3:6-15

GREED
>James 4:1-17

GUILT
>Psalm 32:1,2
>Romans 8:1-17
>Colossians 2:9-17
>1 John 3:11-24

HABITS
>1 John 3:1-24

HAPPINESS
>Matthew 5:1-12
>1 Timothy 6:3-10

HEAVEN
>John 14:1-14
>Colossians 3:1-17

HELL
>Matthew 25:41-46
>Romans 1:18-32
>Revelation 20:1-15

HELP
>Psalm 46:1-11
>Galatians 6:1-10

HOMOSEXUALITY
>Romans 1:18-32
>1 Corinthians 6:9-11
>1 Timothy 1:1-11

HOPE
>Romans 5:1-11
>1 Thessalonians 4:13-18

HURT
>Psalm 55:22
>Psalm 56:3,4
>Psalm 121:1-8
>1 Peter 5:7

IMMORALITY
>1 Corinthians 6:1-20
>Revelation 9:13-21

INDECISIVENESS
>John 3:22-36

INFERIORITY
>Psalm 63:3
>Psalm 86:13
>Psalm 139:13-16
>1 Corinthians 1:26-29
>1 Peter 2:9-10

INSULT
>Proverbs 12:1-28

INTEGRITY
>Psalm 25:1-22
>Luke 16:1-15

JEALOUSY
Romans 13:1-14

JUDGING
Matthew 7:1-6
1 Corinthians 5:1-13

KINDNESS
Luke 6:27-36
Colossians 3:1-17

LAZINESS
2 Thessalonians 3:6-15
2 Peter 3:1-18

LIFESTYLE
Matthew 5:1-12
1 Corinthians 9:1-27
2 Timothy 2:14-26

LONELINESS
Psalm 23:1-6
Isaiah 41:10
Matthew 28:20
Hebrews 13:5,6

LUST
Mark 7:20-23
Romans 6:12
1 Thessalonians 4:3-8
James 1:14,15

LYING
Proverbs 17:20
Proverbs 19:9
Proverbs 24:24
Proverbs 29:12
Proverbs 26:28
Matthew 5:37
Ephesians 4:17-32

MATERIALISM
Matthew 6:19-24

MORALITY
Romans 2:1-16
Romans 12:1-8

MOTIVES
Jeremiah 17:1-18
James 4:1-12

MURDER
Deuteronomy 5:1-33
James 5:1-6

OBEDIENCE
Deuteronomy 30:11-19
Romans 5:1-21

OCCULT
Deuteronomy 18:9-13
1 Samuel 28:7-12
2 Kings 21:6
Isaiah 47:13,14
Acts 19:18-20

PAIN
Hebrews 12:1-13

PEACE
Psalm 3:1-8
John 14:1-31
Romans 5:1-11

PRIORITIES
Proverbs 3:1-35
Matthew 6:25-34

PROBLEMS
James 1:1-18

PROCRASTiNATION

Proverbs 10:1-32
Proverbs 26:1-28

QUARRELS

Proverbs 13:1-10
Titus 3:1-11
James 4:1-12

RELATIONSHIPS

2 Corinthians 6:14-18
Ephesians 2:11-22

RESENTMENT

James 1:1-27

REVENGE

Romans 12:17-21

RIGHTEOUSNESS

Psalm 51:1-19
2 Corinthians 5:11-21

SELF-CENTEREDNESS

Mark 8:31-38
1 Peter 1:14-25

SELFISHNESS

Mark 8:31-38
James 4:1-10

SEX

Proverbs 5:15-21
1 Corinthians 7:1-11
1 Thessalonians 4:1-8

SICKNESS

Psalm 41:3
Psalm 103:3
Matthew 4:23
John 11:4
James 5:13-15

SIN

Isaiah 53:5,6
Isaiah 59:1,2
John 8:34
Romans 3:23
Romans 6:23
Galatians 6:7,8

STRESS

Romans 5:1-5
Philippians 4:4-9

SUFFERING

Romans 8:18
2 Corinthians 1:5
Philippians 3:10
2 Timothy 2:12
James 1:2-8
1 Peter 1:6,7

SUICIDE

Job 14:5
Romans 14:7
1 Corinthians 6:19,20
James 4:7

TEMPTATION

Psalm 94:17-18
Proverbs 28:13
1 Corinthians 10:12,13
Hebrews 4:14-16
James 1:2-14

TERMINAL ILLNESS

Jeremiah 29:11
2 Corinthians 12:9
1 Thessalonians 5:18
2 Timothy 2:12

THANKFULNESS
> Psalm 92:1-15
> Romans 1:18-23
> Ephesians 2:1-10

UNPARDONABLE SIN
> Matthew 12:31,32
> Mark 3:28,29

WAITING
> Psalm 27:1-14
> Psalm 40:1-4
> Matthew 24:32-51

WEAKNESSES
> 2 Corinthians 12:1-10
> 1 John 3:1-11

WILL OF GOD
> Psalm 37:4
> Psalm 91:1,2
> Proverbs 3:5,6
> Proverbs 4:26
> Romans 14:5
> Galatians 6:4
> Ephesians 5:15-21
> Philippians 2:12,13
> 1 Thessalonians 4:3
> 1 Peter 3:17

WISDOM
> Psalm 119:97-112
> Proverbs 1:1-7
> Ecclesiastes 8:1-8
> Luke 2:33-40
> James 1:2-8

WORRY
> Psalm 37:1-11
> Matthew 6:25-34
> Philippians 4:4-9

Bibliography

Adams, Jay E. *Christ And Your Problems*. Nutley, NJ: Presbyterian and Reformed Publishing Company, 1971.

_____. *Competent to Counsel*. Phillipsburg, NJ: Presbyterian and Reformed Publishing Company, 1970.

_____. *Coping With Counseling Crisis*. Grand Rapids, MI: Baker Book House, 1976.

_____. *How to Help People Change*. Grand Rapids, MI: Zondervan Publishing Company, 1986.

_____. *Insight and Creativity in Christian Counseling*. Phillipsburg, NJ: Presbyterian and Reformed Publishing Company, 1982.

_____. *What About Nouthetic Counseling?* Grand Rapids, MI: Baker Book House, 1976.

_____. *The War Within*, Eugene, OR: Harvest House Publishers, 1989.

_____. *The Christian Counselor's Manual*. Phillipsburg, NJ: Presbyterian and Reformed Publishing Company, 1973.

_____. *Update on Christian Counseling Vol. I*. Grand Rapids, MI: Baker Book House, 1980.

Adams, Lane. *How Come It Is Taking So Long to Get Better?* Wheaton, IL: Tyndale House Publishers, Inc., 1975.

Adler, Alfred. *Understanding Human Nature*. New York: Fawcett Premier Books, 1927.

Ahlem, Lloyd H. *How to Cope With Conflict and Change*. Glendale, CA: Regal Books, 1978.

Alexander, Franz. *The History of Psychiatry*, New York: Harper and Row Publishers, 1966.

Anthony, Robert. *50 Ideas That Can Change Your Life!* New York: Berkley Books, 1982.

Augsburger, David. *When Enough Is Enough*. Ventura, CA: Regal Books, 1984.

Backus, William. *Telling Each Other the Truth*. Minneapolis, MN: Bethany House Publishers, 1985.

Barrett, Roger. *Depression—What It Is and What to Do About It*. Elgin, IL: David C. Cook Publishing Company, 1977.

291

Beck, Aaron. *Feeling Good.* New York: William Morrow and Company, Inc., 1980.

Bliss, Edwin. *Doing It Now.* New York: Bantam Books, 1983.

Brande, Dorothea. *Wake Up and Live!* New York: Cornerstone Library, 1968.

Brandt, Henry. *When You're Tired of Treating the Symptoms, and You're Ready for a Cure, Give Me a Call.* Brentwood, TN: Wolgemuth and Hyatt Publishers, Inc., 1991.

Brewer, Ray. *Three Case Studies*—handout, Fresno, CA: California State University, 1978.

Brooks, Michael. *Instant Rapport.* New York: Warner Books, Inc., 1989.

Bruner, Kurt D. *Responsible Living in an Age of Excuses,* Chicago: Moody Press, 1992.

Bulkley, Edward. *Why Christians Can't Trust Psychology,* Eugene, OR: Harvest House Publishers, 1994.

Burns, David. *The Feeling Good Handbook.* New York: Plume Books, 1989.

Cammer, Leonard. *Up From Depression.* New York: Pocket Books, 1969.

Carlson, Dwight L. *Living God's Will.* Old Tappan, NJ: Fleming H. Revell Company, 1976.

Carlson, Dwight, and Wood, Susan Carlson. *When Life Isn't Fair.* Eugene, OR: Harvest House Publishers, 1989.

Carter-Scott, Cherie. *Negaholics.* New York: Fawcett Crest, 1989.

Clark, Robert. *Mental Illness in Perspective.* Pacific Grove, CA: The Boxwood Press, 1973.

Collins, Gary R. *Christian Counseling.* Waco, TX: Word Books, 1980.

_____. *How to Be a People Helper.* Santa Ana, CA: Vision House Publishers, 1976.

Cosgrove, Mark P. *Psychology Gone Awry.* Grand Rapids, MI: Zondervan Publishing House, 1979.

Covan, Frederick L. *Crazy All the Time on the Psych Ward of Bellevue Hospital,* New York: Fawcett Crest, 1994.

Crabb, Larry. *Effective Biblical Counseling.* Grand Rapids, MI: Zondervan Publishing House, 1977.

_____. *Understanding People.* Grand Rapids, MI: Zondervan Publishing House, 1987.

_____. *Inside Out,* Colorado Springs, CO: NavPress, 1988.

Dalbey, Gordon. *Healing the Masculine Soul.* Waco, TX: Word Books, 1988.

Davis, Ron Lee. *The Healing Choice.* Waco, TX: Word Books, 1986.

Demaray, Donald. *Laughter, Joy, and Healing.* Grand Rapids, MI: Baker Book House, 1986.

Dickinson, Richard W. and Page, Carole Gift. *The Child in Each of Us.* Wheaton, IL: Victor Books, 1989.

Diehm, William J. *6 Sure Ways to Solve Any Problem No Matter What,* Nashville, TN: Broadman & Holman Publishers, 1994.

Dobson, James. *Emotions: Can You Trust Them?* Ventura, CA: Regal Books, 1980.

Dotts, Nancy. *Loneliness: Living Between the Times.* Wheaton, IL: Victor Books, 1978.

Dreikurs, Rudolf. *Fundamentals of Adlerian Psychology.* Chicago, IL: Alfred Adler Institute, 1933.

Ellis, Albert, and Harper, Robert A. *A Guide to Rational Living.* North Hollywood, CA: Wilshire Book Company, 1961.

Evans, Stephen C. *Despair.* Downers Grove, IL: InterVarsity Press, 1971.

Eysenck, Hans J. *The Effects of Psychotherapy,* New York: International Science Press, 1966.

_____. *Decline and Fall of The Freudian Empire,* New York: Penguin Books, 1985.

_____. and Nichols, Betty. *"I Do!"* New York: World Almanac Publications, 1985.

Ferguson, Ben. *God, I've Got A Problem.* Santa Ana, CA: Vision House, 1974.

Fisher, Roger, and Ury, William. *Getting to Yes.* New York: Penguin Books, 1981.

Fronk, Ron L. *Creating a Lifestyle You Can Live With.* Springdale, PA: Whitaker House, 1988.

Gillespie, Peggy Roggenbuck, and Bechtel, Lynn. *Less Stress in 30 Days.* New York.

Girdano, Daniel, and Everly, George. *Controlling Stress and Tension.* Englewood Cliffs, NJ: Prentice-Hall, 1979.

Glasser, William. *Control Therapy.* New York: Harper and Row Publishers, 1985.

_____. *Mental Health or Mental Illness.* New York: Harper and Row, Publishers, 1970.

_____. *Reality Therapy.* New York: Harper And Row, Publishers, 1965.

Goddard, Hazel B. *I've Got That Hopeless, Caged In Feeling.* Wheaton, IL: Tyndale House Publishers, 1971.

Goodman, Gerald, and Esterly, Glenn. *The Talk Book.* New York: Ballantine Books, 1988.

Graham, Billy. *The Christian Workers Handbook.* Minneapolis, MN: World Wide, 1981.

Greist, John H. and Jefferson, James W. *Depression and Its Treatment.* New York: Warner Books, 1984.

Haggai, John Edmund. *How to Win Over Worry.* Eugene, OR: Harvest House Publishers, 1987.

_____. *How to Win Over Loneliness.* Eugene, OR: Harvest House Publishers, 1988.

Halper, Jan. *Quiet Desperation.* New York: Warner Books, 1988.

Hansel, Tim. *Eating Problems for Breakfast.* Dallas, TX: Word Publishing , 1988.

Hanson, Peter G. *The Joy of Stress*. Kansas City, KS: Andrews and McNeel, 1987.

Hart, Archibald D. *Adrenalin and Stress*. Waco, Texas: Word Books, 1986.

_____. *Feeling Free*. Old Tappan, NJ: Fleming H. Revell, 1979.

_____. *Unlocking the Mystery of Your Emotions*, Dallas, TX: Word Publishing, 1989.

Hefley, James C. *A Dictionary of Illustrations*, Grand Rapids, MI: Zondervan Publishing House, 1971.

Helmstetter, Shad. *Choices*. New York: Pocket Books, 1989.

Herink, Richie. *The Psychotherapy Handbook*, New York: Meridian Books, 1980.

Hocker, Joyce, and Wilmot, William W. *Interpersonal Conflict*. Dubuque, IA: Wm. C. Brown Publishers, 1978.

Howard, J. Grant, *Knowing God's Will and Doing It!* Grand Rapids, MI: Zondervan Publishing House, 1976.

Hulme, William E. *Creative Loneliness*. Minneapolis, MN: Augsburg Publishing House, 1977.

Jackson, Edgar. *Understanding Loneliness*. Philadelphia: Fortress Press, 1980.

Jauncey, James H. *Above Ourselves*. Grand Rapids, MI: Zondervan Publishing House, 1964.

Jeremiah, David. *Overcoming Loneliness*. San Bernardino, CA: Here's Life Publishers, Inc., 1983.

Jones, Brian G., and Phillips-Jones, Linda. *Men Have Feelings Too*. Wheaton, IL: Victor Books, 1988.

Journal of Consulting Psychology. *The Effects Of Psychotherapy: An Evaluation*, Volume 16, Number 5, October 1952.

Jung, C. G. *Memories, Dreams, Reflections*. New York: Vintage Books, 1989.

Kaminer, Wendy. *I'm Dysfunctional, You're Dysfunctional*. New York: Vintage Books, 1992.

Keating, Paul. *Emotions and Mental Health*. New Canaan, CT: Keats Publishing, Inc., 1975.

LaHaye, Tim, and Phillips, Bob. *Anger Is a Choice*. Grand Rapids, MI: Zondervan Publishing House, 1982.

LaHaye, Tim. *How to Win Over Depression*. Grand Rapids, MI: Zondervan Publishing House, 1974.

Lane, Allen. *Museums of Madness*. London, England: Penguin Books, 1979.

Lindquist, Stanley. *Action Helping Skills*. Fresno, CA: Link-Care Foundation Press, 1976.

Losoncy, Lewis. *Turning People On*. New York: Prentice Hall Press, 1977.

Lum, Doman. *Responding to Suicidal Crisis*. Grand Rapids, MI: William B. Eerdmans Publishing Company, 1977.

Lutzer, Erwin. *How to Say No to a Stubborn Habit*. Wheaton, IL: Victor Books, 1979.

_____. *Managing Your Emotions*. Chappaqua, New York: Christian Herald Books, 1981.

MacArthur, John. *God's Will Is Not Lost*. Wheaton, IL: Victor Books, 1973.

Mallory, James D. *The Kink and I*. Grand Rapids, MI: Zondervan Publishing House, 1973.

Masson, Jeffrey Moussaieff. *Against Therapy*, Atheneum, NY: 1988.

Marsh, Peter. *Eye to Eye*. Topsfield, MA: Salem House Publishers, 1988.

McMillen, S.I. *None of These Diseases*, Westwood, NJ: Spire Books, 1963.

Miller, Sherod; Wackerman, Daniel; Nunnally, Elam; and Saline, Carol. *Straight Talk*. New York: Signet Books, 1981.

Minirth, Frank B. and Meier, Paul D. *Happiness Is a Choice*. Grand Rapids, MI: Baker Book House, 1978.

Moorehead, Bob. *Counsel Yourself & Others from the Bible*, Sisters, OR: Multnomah Books, 1994.

Murphree, Jon Tal. *When God Says You're OK*. Downers Grove, IL: InterVarsity Press, 1976.

Neff, Miriam. *Women and Their Emotions*. Chicago, IL: Moody Press, 1983.

Peck, M. Scott. *The Road Less Traveled*, New York: Touchstone Books, 1978.

Perry, Lloyd M., and Sell, Charles M. *Speaking to Life's Problems*. Chicago, IL: Moody Press, 1983.

Podrabinek, Alexander. *Punitive Medicine*. Ann Arbor, MI: Karoma Publishers, 1980.

Pokras, Sandy. Systematic *Problem-Solving And Decision Making*. Los Altos, CA: Crisp Publications, Inc., 1989.

Porter, Roy. *A Social History of Madness*, New York: Weidenfeld & Nicoloson, 1987.

Potthoff, Harvey H. *Understanding Loneliness*. New York: Harper and Row Publishers, 1976.

Prater, Arnold. *How to Beat the Blahs*. Irvine, CA: Harvest House Publishers, 1977.

Rohrer, Norman B. and Sutherland, S. Philip. *Why Am I Shy?* Minneapolis: Augsburg Publishing House, 1978.

Rosellini, Gayle, and Worden, Mark. *Of Course You're Anxious*. New York: Harper San Francisco, 1990.

Rubin, Theodore Isaac. *Overcoming Indecisiveness*. New York: Avon Books, 1985.

Schlenger, Sunny, and Roesch, Roberta. *How to Be Organized in Spite of Yourself*. New York: Signet Books, 1989.

Schmidt, Kenneth. *Finding Your Way Home*. Ventura, CA: Regal Books, 1990.

Scott, Gini Graham. *Resolving Conflict*. Oakland, CA: New Harbinger Publications, Inc., 1990.

Sehnert, Keith W. *Stress and Unstress*. Minneapolis: Augsburg Publishing House, 1981.

Semands, David. *Healing for Damaged Emotions*. Wheaton, IL: Victor Books, 1981.

Smedes, Lewis B. *Forgive and Forget*. New York: Pocket Books, 1984.

Solomon, Charles R. *Counselling With the Mind of Christ*. Old Tappan, NJ: Fleming H. Revell Company, 1977.

_____. *Handbook of Happiness*. Denver, CO: House of Solomon, 1971.

Steiner, Claude. *Scripts People Live*. New York: Bantam Books, 1974.

Szasz, Thomas S. *The Manufacture of Madness*. New York: Harper and Row Publishers, 1977.

_____. *Insanity*. New York: John Wiley & Sons, 1987.

_____. *The Myth of Mental Illness*. New York: Harper Colophon Books, 1974.

_____. *Anti-Freud*. Syracuse University Press, 1976.

_____. *The Myth of Psycho Therapy*. Garden City, NY: Anchor Books, 1979.

_____. *Schizophrenia*. New York: Syracuse University Press, 1976.

_____. *The Untamed Tongue*. LaSalle, IL, Open Court: 1990.

_____. *The Therapeutic State*. Buffalo, NY: Prometheus Books, 1984.

_____. *Cruel Compassion*. New York: John Wiley & Sons, Inc. 1994.

Umphrey, Marjorie, and Laird, Richard. *Why I Don't Feel OK?* Irvine, CA: Harvest House Publishers, 1977.

Viscott, David. *The Language of Feelings*. New York: Pocket Books, 1976.

_____. *The Viscott Method*. New York: Pocket Books, 1984.

VonOech, Roger. *A Kick in the Seat of the Pants*. New York: Harper and Row Publishers, 1986.

_____. *A Whack in the Side of the Head*. New York: Harper And Row Publishers, 1983.

Wahlroos, Suen. *Excuses*. New York: Macmillan Publishing Company, Inc., 1981.

Walsh, Thomas A. *Beyond Psychology*. Eaugallie, FL: Harbour House, 1990.

Walters, Candace. *Invisible Wounds*. Portland, OR: Multnomah Press, 1987.

Whybrow, Peter, and Bahr, Robert. *The Hibernation Response*. New York: Avon Books, 1988.

Wood, Garth. *The Myth of Neurosis*. New York: Harper and Row Publishers, 1983.

Wright, H. Norman. *The Christian Use of Emotional Power*. Old Tappan, NJ: Fleming H. Revell, 1974.

_____. *An Answer to Anger and Frustration*. Irvine, CA: Harvest House Publishers, 1977.

_____. *An Answer to Loneliness*. Irvine, CA: Harvest House Publishers, 1977.

Yancey, Philip. *Where Is God When It Hurts?* Grand Rapids, MI: Zondervan Publishing House, 1977.

Zimbardo, Philip G. *Shyness*. Reading, MA: Addison-Wesley Publishing Company, Inc., 1977.
Zois, Christ. *Think Like a Shrink*. New York: Warner Books, 1992.

Notes

Chapter 1—Am I Crazy?

1. Ray Brewer, *Three Case Studies*—a handout (Fresno, CA: California State University, 1978).

Chapter 2—The Myth of Mental Illness

1. Thomas Szasz, *The Therapeutic State* (Buffalo, NY: Prometheus Books, 1984), pp. 137-46.
2. Ibid., pp. 147-54.

Chapter 3—Sitting on a Tack

1. C.G. Jung, *Memories, Dreams, Reflections* (New York: Vintage Books, 1989), p. 30.
2. Ibid., p. 31.
3. Ibid., pp. 31-32.
4. *Journal of Consulting Psychology*, "The Effects Of Psychotherapy: An Evaluation," vol. 16, no. 5, Oct. 1952, pp. 319-24.
5. Hans J. Eysenck, *The Effects of Psychotherapy* (New York: International Science Press, 1966), p. 94.
6. Edward Bulkley, *Why Christians Can't Trust Psychology* (Eugene, OR: Harvest House Publishers, 1994), pp. 57-76.
7. Garth Wood, *The Myth of Neurosis* (New York: Harper and Row, Publishers, 1983), p. 286.
8. Jay E. Adams, *Competent to Counsel* (Phillipsburg, NJ: Presbyterian and Reformed Publishing Company, 1970), p. 21.

Chapter 4—Cain—The Father of Mental Illness

1. Adapted from Frank B. Minirth and Paul D. Meier, *Happiness Is a Choice* (Grand Rapids, MI: Baker Book House, 1978), pp. 28-29.

Chapter 5—Where There's Smoke, There's Fire

1. If you would like more information about how to deal with the emotion of anger, look for the book entitled *Anger Is a Choice*. It can be picked up at your local bookstore or by writing Family Services at P.O. Box 9363, Fresno, CA 93792.
2. Adapted from Tim LaHaye and Bob Phillips, *Anger Is a Choice* (Grand Rapids, MI: Zondervan Publishing House, 1982), pp. 46-49.

Chapter 9—Understanding Yourself and Others

1. If you would like more details about Social Styles and how to get along with people, look for the book entitled *The Delicate Art of Dancing With Porcupines*. It can be picked up at your local bookstore or by writing Family Services at P.O. Box 9363, Fresno, CA 93702.

Chapter 10—The Hardest Thing to Do in Life

1. S. I. McMillen, *None of These Diseases* (Westwood, NJ: Spire Books, 1963), pp. 73-74.

Chapter 12—Doing Away With Ulcers

1. James C. Hefley, *A Dictionary of Illustrations* (Grand Rapids, MI: Zondervan Publishing House, 1971), p. 126.
2. Adapted from *Attitude: Your Most Priceless Possession* (Los Altos, CA: Crisp Publications, Inc.).

Index

Other Books
by Bob Phillips

WIT AND WISDOM

THE GREAT BIBLE CHALLENGE

HOW CAN I BE SURE?

ANGER IS A CHOICE

REDI-REFERENCE

*REDI-REFERENCE DAILY
BIBLE READING PLAN*

*THE DELICATE ART OF DANCING
WITH PORCUPINES*

GOD'S HAND OVER HUME

*PRAISE IS A THREE-LETTERED
WORD—JOY*

FRIENDSHIP, LOVE & LAUGHTER

PHILLIPS' BOOK OF GREAT QUOTES & FUNNY SAYINGS

THE ALL-AMERICAN QUOTE BOOK

*BIG BOOK—THE BIBLE—QUESTIONS
AND ANSWERS*

For information on how to purchase any of the above books or any other
book by Bob Phillips, contact your local bookstore or send a
self-addressed stamped envelope to:
Family Services
P.O. Box 9363
Fresno, CA 93702